The Edible Woman

The Edible Woman

By Dave Carley

Based on the novel by **Margaret Atwood**

The Edible Woman
first published 2002 by
Scirocco Drama
An imprint of J. Gordon Shillingford Publishing Inc.
© 1999-2000 Dave Carley
Based upon the novel by Margaret Atwood

Scirocco Drama Editor: Glenda MacFarlane
Cover design by Scott Thornley + Company Inc.
Author photo by Michael Lee
Printed and bound in Canada

We acknowledge the financial support of The Canada Council for the Arts
and the Manitoba Arts Council for our publishing program.

Production inquiries should be addressed to:
Patricia Ney, Christopher Banks and Associates
6 Adelaide Street, Suite 610
Toronto, Ontario, Canada M5C 1H6
(416) 214-1155
cbanks@pathcom.com

Canadian Cataloguing in Publication Data

Carley, Dave, 1955-
    The Edible woman

A play, based on the novel by Margaret Atwood.
ISBN 1-896239-84-6
    I. Title.
PS8555.A7397E35 2002   C812'.54   C2002-900247-8
PR9199.3.C337E35 2002

J. Gordon Shillingford Publishing
P.O. Box 86, 905 Corydon Avenue, Winnipeg, MB Canada R3M 3S3

Acknowledgments

Special thanks to: Margaret Atwood, Timothy Bond, Heather Brown, CanStage, CBC Radio Arts and Entertainment, Sara Chazen, Mary Lou Chlipala, Frank Gagliano, Phoebe Larmore, Glynis Leyshon, Glenda MacFarlane, Christopher McHarge, Elaine Merritt, the Michigan Festival of New Works, Susan Murray, Theatre on the Grand, Gordon Shillingford, Molly Thom, Iris Turcott, The Vancouver Playhouse, and Michael Waller. Also, to the participants in a June 2001 workshop at CanStage: Raoul Bhaneja, Rebecca Brown, Loretta Bailey, Timothy Bond, Paul Essiembre, Ellen-Ray Hennessey, Katherine Kaszas, Stephen Ouimette, Tara Samuel, Iris Turcott, and Michael Waller. And to the cast of the Vancouver Playhouse/CanStage production: Jillian Fargey, Ellen-Ray Hennessey, Darren Keay, Alec McClure, Tara Samuel, Haig Sutherland and Todd Talbot.

Dave Carley

Dave Carley is the author of a number of works for stage, including *Writing With Our Feet*, *A View From the Roof*, *After You* (Scirocco Drama, 1995) and *Walking on Water* (Signature Editions, 2000). He has been nominated for the Governor General's Award for Drama and is a three-time Chalmers Award finalist. He received the 2000 Arthur Miller Playwriting Award from the University of Michigan and has been the playwright-in-residence at Ontario's Stratford Festival and Barrington Stage Company in Massachusetts. Dave was born and raised in Peterborough, Ontario and now lives in Toronto where he is senior script editor for CBC Radio drama. For more information, his website is www.davecarley.com

Cast

MARIAN McAlpin: age 25
AINSLEY Tewce: age 25
LEN Slank: age 27, feigned English accent.
PETER Wollander: age 26
DUNCAN: age 26, but looks younger.
LUCY: the Office Virgin (35), can double with TREVOR (30) and
with LANDLADY (50)

Time and Place

Toronto, 1965.

Act I: Labour Day weekend—start of September
Act II: The months following

Set and Staging

The set must be flexible, to allow set-pieces to roll, slide, drop in or
pop up.

In the first act, MARIAN almost always moves the set-pieces
herself. In the second act, the changes are entirely out of her control
until near the end of the play.

MARIAN often speaks directly to the audience. These speeches
are marked (*To Audience.*) In Act I they generally occur when she is
moving a set-piece about.

Sentences ending (in brackets) indicate that the subsequent
speaker should override the bracketed words.

Production History

The Edible Woman was originally dramatized for radio, and was first broadcast on CBC Sunday Showcase, Monday Night Playhouse and This Morning in 1996. The cast included Martha Burns (Marian), Ann-Marie Macdonald (Ainsley), Michael Riley (Peter) and Albert Schultz (Len Slank). Heather Brown was Producer.

The stage version of *The Edible Woman* was workshopped by Theatre on the Grand, in Fergus and Toronto, in February, 2000. Chris McHarge directed. The actors were Burgandy Code, Jim Jones, Darren Keay, Elisa Moolecherry, Tara Samuel and Brendan Wall.

The Edible Woman was first presented at the Festival of New Works at the University of Michigan, Ann Arbor, in May 2000. The cast consisted of Cecily Smith (Marian), Julia Siple (Ainsley), James Meade (Len Slank), Casey Murphy (Peter), Michael Messer (Duncan) and Nona Gerard (Lucy, Trevor and Landlady.) Director was Sara Chazen. Stage Manager was Nancy Uffner. Lighting: Mark Berg. Sound: Nate Cartier. The Festival's Artistic Director is Frank Gagliano and its Producing Director is Mary Lou Chlipala.

The Edible Woman premiered at Theatre on the Grand in Fergus, Ontario, on October 5, 2000, with the following cast and crew:

PETER .... Steven Guy-McGrath
MARIAN .... Kate Hemblen
DUNCAN .... Darren Keay
AINSLEY .... Kim Kuhteubl
LEN .... Michael Waller
LANDLADY/LUCY/TREVOR .... Marjorie Wingrove

Director: Christopher McHarge
Associate Director: Michael Waller
Set Design by Christopher Haupt
Lighting Design by Karen Bayer
Stage Manager: Bill Brillinger
Assistant Stage Manager: Eric Goudie

Act One

The skyline of a modern city. As the lights dim, the skyline reduces, the skyscrapers of today giving way to the lower-rise buildings of three decades ago. The sounds of crisp lovemaking are established. Lights rise on PETER's apartment. All that is visible is a bathtub and then a portion of PETER's bottom having efficient sex. MARIAN appears, fully dressed, and perches on the edge of the tub.

MARIAN: *(To Audience.)* Peter and I met at a garden party. He was a friend of a friend. Of a friend. People notice my Peter. Oh, not because he has forceful or peculiar features. But because he is—how can I put this—ordinariness raised to perfection. My roommate Ainsley calls him "nicely packaged", but I don't think she means that in a positive way. Peter never sheds. And he never shines in the wrong places.

(Holds PETER's face up for Audience.) Sometimes I want a reassuring wart or mole. *(Puts PETER's face back down again.)* He's almost a lawyer. He's rising at his firm, like a hot air balloon.

MARIAN eases herself into the tub with PETER, as he soldiers on. MARIAN, however, is never really in a plausible sexual position with PETER—and he never notices. She continues talking.

(To Audience.) My Peter lives in a nearly-completed high-rise named after a western province. The Manitoba. Making love in the tub is his idea. Actually I don't think it's a good one. The tub's

small and ridgy—but when you care for someone—
and I do care for Peter—well, you make little
bathtub-type sacrifices, don't you.

*Moderate concluding sigh from PETER, which
promptly elicits a sympathetic, echoing, moderate,
concluding sigh from MARIAN.*

PETER: How was it for you?

MARIAN: Marvellous.

PETER: Good.

MARIAN: Really marvellous.

            Pause.

            Peter.

PETER: Mmm.

MARIAN: Peter, what would you say if I said, "rotten"?

            PETER laughs, a little nervously.

            You wouldn't believe me, would you.

            PETER laughs, a little nervously.

            It wasn't.

PETER: Wasn't what, dear?

MARIAN: Wasn't rotten. Peter?

PETER: Mmm?

MARIAN: Why did we just make love in the bathtub? Were we
            being reckless? Or do you see me as just another
            lavatory fixture?

PETER: I really get a kick out of you sometimes. You want to
            do it again?

MARIAN: I'd love to but it's awfully late.

            MARIAN gets out of tub.

PETER: Is it?

              MARIAN starts to get back in tub.

MARIAN: Isn't it?

PETER: Maybe it is.

              MARIAN is back and forthing.

MARIAN: I mean, I could stay—over—

PETER: If you like—

MARIAN: *(The rule:)* But it's a weeknight.

PETER: *(Relieved.)* Yes, it is.

MARIAN: You always say Fridays at the office are the worst.

PETER: True. Fridays and Mondays. Living hell.

MARIAN: And I know you can go all night but I need my beauty sleep.

              MARIAN pushes or sends PETER—still in the tub—offstage.

              Anyway, I'm seeing you tomorrow night, we can try it in the kitchen sink.

PETER: I'm going to hold you to that.

MARIAN: I'm rather afraid you will. Peter, would you mind terribly—

PETER: Drive you home? Sure thing—just let me get dressed. I can drop by the Morissey on my way back—make last call with Trigger. He sounded morose—

              MARIAN has pushed PETER off and returns, pushing her own bed into place.

MARIAN: *(To Audience.)* Home is a flat I share with Ainsley. I met her through a friend, of a friend, and then through another friend we both got jobs at Seymour

Surveys. That's an awful lot of Ainsley.

MARIAN lies back.

(To Audience.) But we get along by a symbiotic adjustment of habits and with a minimum of—of that pale-mauve hostility you so often find among women.

Alarm rings. MARIAN sits up.

(To Audience.) I swear I didn't sleep a wink. But I'm feeling all right. In fact, I'm feeling even more stolid than usual. Just a bit ridgy.

MARIAN takes a big bite of her toast. AINSLEY enters, with a glass of tomato juice. She is still in her robe and nursing an obvious hangover.

You look awful!

AINSLEY: I feel awful!

MARIAN: It must have been a great party.

AINSLEY: Au contraire. There was no one there but dentistry students, so I had to get drunk. A room-full of conversations about the insides of people's mouths. The only reaction I got all night was when I described that abcess I had. They drooled.

AINSLEY lies down. MARIAN gets out of bed. She is fully dressed, ready for work.

MARIAN: You need alka seltzer. Juice. Toast. Fiddlesticks—look at (the time)

AINSLEY: I bet they all carry those bent mirrors and peer into their own mouths every time they go to the john, to make sure they're still cavity-free.

MARIAN: The bus is in three minutes!

MARIAN starts handing AINSLEY her clothes. She continues to eat. AINSLEY continues to talk and to reject MARIAN's ideas for her work outfit.

AINSLEY: Can you imagine kissing a dentist?

MARIAN: Hurry!

AINSLEY: He'd say, "Open Wide".

MARIAN: Couldn't you have changed the topic?

AINSLEY: Of course not. I pretended to be terribly interested. But I'm off dentists now. Life is so disappointing. Last year I thought I'd fall in love with an actor.

MARIAN: Until you started meeting some.

AINSLEY: I'm going to get a job in one of those little galleries and meet a bona fide artist.

MARIAN: Those little galleries don't pay well. (Wear this.)

AINSLEY: Could it be any less than the pittance I get at Seymour?

MARIAN: It could be a lot less. (What about this?)

AINSLEY: A life spent tabulating surveys. What else does one do with a B.A. these days?

MARIAN mouths the last line with AINSLEY— she's heard it many times before.

No, that dress—that one—

MARIAN hands AINSLEY an orange dress.

MARIAN: You want to wear this?

AINSLEY: Why not.

MARIAN: Isn't it a bit orange?

AINSLEY: Unlike you, I don't wear clothes for camouflage.

MARIAN: Camouflage!

AINSLEY: Protective colouration.

MARIAN: That's not fair. Ainsley, do something with your hair.

AINSLEY: I can't.

MARIAN: Close the door behind you or Landlady will have
             something to say.

AINSLEY: The old bitch always has something to say.

             *AINSLEY and MARIAN turn. LANDLADY is
             waiting for them.*

LANDLADY: Good morning Miss McAlpin.

MARIAN: I uh—isn't this humidity dreadful—

LANDLADY: I was out last night. At a meeting.

AINSLEY: *(Sotto.)* Temperance Union.

LANDLADY: The Child—

AINSLEY: *(Sotto.)* The Hulk.

LANDLADY: Pardon me?

MARIAN: You were saying—

LANDLADY: The Child tells me there was another fire.

MARIAN: It wasn't exactly a fire.

LANDLADY: The Child says there was a lot of smoke.

MARIAN: It was just pork chops. I'm sorry.

AINSLEY: Marian, we really must hurry.

LANDLADY: I do wish you would tell Miss Tewce to make less
             smoke in the future. It upsets The Child.

MARIAN: Yes, of course. You'll have to excuse us.

             MARIAN and AINSLEY move past LANDLADY.

             "Less smoke" please, Miss Tewce.

             MARIAN erects a bus-stop pole.

             Oh fiddlesticks. No bus. We're late.

AINSLEY: We're early for the next one. "Less smoke", what the hell's (she on about)

MARIAN: Why doesn't Landlady ever stop you to talk about things? Why's it always me!

AINSLEY: It's your cloak of respectability.

MARIAN: My what?

AINSLEY: You wore gloves the day she interviewed us for the flat. Of course she's going to talk to you.

MARIAN: You must be careful about cooking—

AINSLEY: She's hoping we'll really do something. What she wants is an orgy.

MARIAN: You're paranoid.

AINSLEY: I'll bet she's up in our rooms right now, snooping through our things.

MARIAN: She has a daughter!

AINSLEY: She has a hulk.

MARIAN: Well, even that poor thing needs protection; Landlady has a right to be worried about the smoke. What if the house was on fire? And she's never mentioned the other things.

AINSLEY: What "other things"? We've never done any "other things"!

Sound of bus approaching, under.

MARIAN: There it is.

AINSLEY: Marian: what "other things"?

MARIAN: The bottles.

AINSLEY: We're adults!

AINSLEY is riding the bus—swaying and holding a loop, while MARIAN begins setting up office. She might also be eating peanuts.

Which reminds me—we're out of Scotch. Have you got three dollars? Marian?

MARIAN: What.

AINSLEY: Three dollars? For the Scotch?

MARIAN: Right, right.

> MARIAN pauses in her construction of Seymour Surveys to rummage for money. She gives it to AINSLEY and resumes set-up.

This is slightly unjust.

AINSLEY: Why!

MARIAN: We split the cost fifty-fifty but not the contents.

AINSLEY: Then drink more.

MARIAN: I can't! When I was ten I wrote a temperance essay for a Sunday School competition. Pictures of car crashes, diseased livers in burnt magenta—

AINSLEY: So?

MARIAN: So now I can't take a second drink without a crayon warning sign flashing in my brain. "Take the pledge!"

AINSLEY: You need help. *(Sees LUCY coming.)* Oh oh.

MARIAN: *(With AINSLEY.)* Oh oh.

> AINSLEY moves off but stays within earshot. She is studiously busy when talk of volunteers comes up. LUCY arrives with files, which she passes to MARIAN.

LUCY: Finally.

MARIAN: I'll work late. Did anyone notice?

LUCY: Nothing was mentioned. Though everything is noted. By The Men Upstairs. I tried to cover for you. Anyway, Marian, we have another problem.

MARIAN: Not more rice pudding.

LUCY: Yes, the nutritionist has asked us to sample the new vanilla variations. Open up.

MARIAN groans. But opens up obediently. AINSLEY is very, very busy tabulating.

Vanilla Orange.

MARIAN: *(Indicates it's OK.)*

LUCY: Vanilla Caramel.

MARIAN: *(Indicates it's less OK. She's fed a third sample and reacts:)* That's disgusting.

LUCY: Vanilla Pumpkin Swirl. Ainsley?

AINSLEY: Hangover.

LUCY: *(Back to MARIAN.)* I'm afraid it's more than the pudding. We're running the beer study next week and The Men Upstairs decided we need to do a pre-test this weekend. The Men Upstairs are worried about your questionnaire.

MARIAN: What's wrong with it!

LUCY: The Men Upstairs think your questions are too simple.

MARIAN: I spent an entire week working on them! I had to turn the convoluted gobbledygook of The Men Upstairs into questions that can be answered by the typical beer drinking 'Man Out There'.

LUCY: I know, I know, Marian, but *(Indicates The Men Upstairs.)* And the thing is, it's the long weekend and all our regular interviewers are "en famille". And I've made plans.

AINSLEY: Really?

LUCY: *(Proudly.)* A man.

MARIAN and AINSLEY react.

	OK. My brother. But you're going to be in town, aren't you?
MARIAN:	Does it have to be this weekend?
LUCY:	We need the results by Tuesday. You only have to find seven or eight male beer drinkers. No one else is free, I've asked.
MARIAN:	I'll do it tomorrow.
LUCY:	We knew we could rely on you.

LUCY leaves, watched by AINSLEY and MARIAN. AINSLEY starts to make a face.

MARIAN:	Be nice. She could've asked you.
AINSLEY:	I'm a mere tabulator.

AINSLEY moves off. MARIAN finds a wafer cookie in her purse.

MARIAN: *(To Audience.)* Seymour Surveys is layered like a wafer cookie. It's got an upper crust, a lower crust, and then there's my department, the uh—the gooey layer in the middle. On the floor above are the executives and psychologists—The Men Upstairs—since they are, in fact, all men. Below us are the Machine People—the operators of the mimeographs, the Gestetners... My floor is the link between. We take care of the human element—Seymour's crack nationwide network of interviewers. Housewives, mostly. I prepare their simple questionnaires. Imagine: hundreds of women asking thousands of Canadians my questions. *(Shrugs.)* To my right is Ainsley, our erstwhile tabulator. To my left is the floor manager, Lucy. The Office Virgin.

The phone begins ringing; LUCY gets it.

(To Audience.) I'm in the middle. The middle of the goo.

LUCY: Marian. It's for you. A young gentleman.

Light up on PETER, who stands off, in suit.

MARIAN:	Seymour Surveys, may (I help you?)
PETER:	Marian?
MARIAN:	Peter?
PETER:	Marian—is that you?
MARIAN:	Yes Peter, it's me.
PETER:	You have your office voice.
MARIAN:	Sorry.
PETER:	Listen Marian, I can't make it for dinner tonight.
MARIAN:	Oh?
PETER:	I know you'll understand. It's Trigger.
MARIAN:	What about Trigger? Is he OK?
PETER:	No, he's not. He's—he's—
MARIAN:	What's happened!?
PETER:	He's getting married.
MARIAN:	Trigger got engaged!
PETER:	Yesterday. At approximately 8:06 p.m.
MARIAN:	Exactly when we were in the bathtub.
PETER:	Just like that. Engaged!
MARIAN:	To that girl?
PETER:	Yes. He's told me everything.
MARIAN:	When?
PETER:	Last night. He managed to make last call at the Morrissey. He stumbled in—I could barely recognize him. I should be with him tonight.
MARIAN:	Would you like me to come with you?

PETER: God no—that would make it even worse. You understand. I'll take you out tomorrow night instead, okay?

                PETER hangs up, then MARIAN. Light off PETER. AINSLEY and LUCY are waiting, expectantly.

MARIAN: That was Peter.

LUCY: We know.

AINSLEY: Is there something wrong?

MARIAN: Trigger's in trouble.

LUCY: Who?

MARIAN: Trigger was Peter's last old friend to remain successfully unmarried. Just before I began dating Peter two of his pals succumbed and in the past six months another three have gone under—without warning.

AINSLEY: Poor Petey. To lose so many, so quickly.

MARIAN: Peter and Trigger were clinging to each other like drowning men. But now Trigger has apparently succumbed. Peter'll need careful handling tomorrow night. I sure hope he doesn't think I'm getting ideas.

LUCY: None of this is fair. I wish I could succumb. *(Leaving.)* Everyone else is succumbing; why can't I. Succumb.

                LUCY leaves.

MARIAN: Say—Ainsley—I suddenly seem to be free tonight— what about you?

AINSLEY: Why.

MARIAN: We could go see Clara.

AINSLEY: I'll take a pass.

MARIAN: We should give her a break from child-rearing.

AINSLEY:	Clara bugs me.
MARIAN:	Ainsley! She introduced us!
AINSLEY:	She just lies there and Joe does all the work! She lets herself be treated like a thing!
MARIAN:	She's seven months pregnant! She's got a four year-old and another babe-in-arms!
AINSLEY:	She should be getting her degree. But oh no, Clara's depending on her husband for everything. You won't ever catch me lying on a lawn chair doing nothing, waiting for some man to make me dinner. *(Counts off months.)* Next summer.

MARIAN has begun moving off the Seymour Surveys set. She brings on an aluminum pole and and she and AINSLEY cling to it and rock. MARIAN might also be testing some pudding. The other actors can also be on the subway car, facing away from the audience, rocking with the car's movement. They will move in, to eavesdrop.

MARIAN:	Lord it's hot for September. Why'd we take the subway? My skin feels like I'm enclosed in a layer of moist dough.
	(To herself.) "You won't catch me..." *(To AINSLEY.)* What did you mean earlier, when you said, "You won't catch me next summer—"
AINSLEY:	Next summer what—
MARIAN:	You said you won't be caught on a lawn chair— "next summer".
AINSLEY:	Oh that. I'm going to have a baby.
MARIAN:	You're going to have a baby.
AINSLEY:	I don't mean I'm already pregnant. I'm going to get pregnant!
MARIAN:	What—you're going to get married?! Don't tell

	Peter. That's about the only thing you two ever agree on—*not* getting married.
AINSLEY:	Of course I'm not getting married! That's what's wrong with most children; they have too many parents. Look at Joe and Clara, her lying there like a sloth and Joe doing all the father and mother work. Think how confused their children's parental images will be! And it's mostly the father's fault.
MARIAN:	Joe's wonderful! Clara couldn't cope without him!
AINSLEY:	Of course she would cope! She'd have to. Have you noticed she isn't even breast-feeding the baby?
MARIAN:	The thing has teeth!
AINSLEY:	So what! I bet Joe put her up to that. North American men hate watching the basic mother-child unit functioning naturally. It makes them feel not needed!
MARIAN:	Keep your voice down. Ainsley, how long have you been thinking about this?
AINSLEY:	Since this morning. I know what I've said about babies in the past. Those are other people's babies. Other people's babies are disgusting. (*As if advertising the ownership of a hairdryer, and for the benefit of the eavesdroppers.*) Every woman should have a baby. At least one. It's even more important than sex. It fulfills your deepest femininity.

A jerk and hiss as subway car stops. MARIAN and AINSLEY get off, and the others disperse. MARIAN immediately starts reconstructing their flat. Piano scales—fractured—can be heard in background.

MARIAN:	Peter says our flat lacks unity.
AINSLEY:	How can that be—everything is yours.
MARIAN:	I guess I must lack unity then.
AINSLEY:	Doesn't that hulking thing ever stop! I'll tell you

this: no child of mine is ever going to study piano.

LANDLADY appears.

LANDLADY: Sshh. The Child is practising.

MARIAN: Sorry.

Bottles clank.

LANDLADY: What was that?

AINSLEY: What was what.

LANDLADY: I heard a clank.

AINSLEY: Pickles.

LANDLADY: Pickles don't clank, Miss Tewce. Liquor clanks.

Scales have stopped in background.

Now look what you've done. The Child has lost her concentration. Coming dear.

LANDLADY exits.

MARIAN: You know, Landlady may not appreciate an illegitimate baby in the house.

AINSLEY: "Illegitimate"? What a bourgeois word! Birth is always legitimate.

MARIAN: And babies do a lot more than clank. Oh, and one more little problem. Who's going to be the father? I know it's just a technical detail, but you will need one of those, if only for a short time. You can't just send out a bud. And I'm not lending Peter.

AINSLEY: God no! Peter (ugh)

MARIAN: He'd be a perfectly good father! What about that dentistry student you dated last night?

AINSLEY: Receding chin.

MARIAN: The randy office boy at Seymour?

AINSLEY: I don't think he's very bright. I'd prefer an artist of course, but that's too risky, genetically. By now they probably all have chromosome breaks from LSD. Much as it displeases me, I may have to begin my search in some of our better nightclubs. Tonight. Now that we're not seeing Clara, and Peter's off mourning with Trigger—you're free, right?

MARIAN: I'm too tired to go to some bar and help you troll the gene pool. Besides, I've got to do the beer survey first thing tomorrow.

AINSLEY: What about tomorrow night?

MARIAN: Peter's taking me out to make up for tonight. Oh fiddlesticks—I'm supposed to have drinks with Len Slank.

AINSLEY: Len who?

MARIAN: Len Slank. A friend from college days. He's just returned from England. Likely deported on some morals charge.

AINSLEY: (Beat.) Tell me more about this Len.

MARIAN: He's not nice really, sort of a seducer of virgins.

AINSLEY: (Makes disgusted sound.)

MARIAN: Anything over seventeen is too old.

AINSLEY: (Makes disgusted sound.)

MARIAN: It's odd, because he doesn't need to. Specialize. I mean, he's quite handsome.

AINSLEY: Oh?

MARIAN: Intelligent, too.

AINSLEY: Really. What does he do?

MARIAN: He's in television—

AINSLEY: Oh?

MARIAN: Don't even think it. Get that thought out of your mind.

AINSLEY: Which thought.

MARIAN: The Len Slank one.

AINSLEY: Why not?

MARIAN: For starters, he only likes virgins.

AINSLEY: I can be that.

MARIAN: He'd be a terrible donor; he's too sleazy.

AINSLEY: Sleaziness is a learned behaviour, not genetic. You don't think I'm serious, do you.

MARIAN: Actually, I'm very much afraid you are.

AINSLEY leaves. MARIAN lies on her bed. Black. An alarm bell promptly rings. MARIAN sits up, waking from dream. She eventually moves out her apartment flat and brings in a door.

(To Audience.) I was just dreaming. My feet were beginning to dissolve into vanilla pumpkin swirl. I put on a pair of rubber boots just in time—only to find that the ends of my fingers were turning transparent. Weird.

(Picks up clipboard.) Time to survey the city's beer drinkers.

At the door, MARIAN goes to knock. She stops, straightens her dress, makes an "official" face. She knocks.

(To Audience.) It always amazes me that people consent to be interviewed when they don't get paid.

Knocks.

(To Audience.) Maybe they just need someone to talk to.

Knocks.

(To Audience.) Or they're flattered someone is finally asking their opinion on something.

The door swings open.

Hello? Hello? Is anyone—hello?

DUNCAN appears, in a bathrobe, holding an iron.

Hello there. Is your father in?

DUNCAN: *(Pause.)* No. He's dead. *(Pause.)* What do you want?

MARIAN: I'm doing a survey but you have to be—oh. Are you—how old are you?

DUNCAN: *(Pause.)* Twenty-six.

MARIAN: Twenty-six! That's fine. I'm from Seymour Surveys. Here's our card. I'm not selling anything but I am interested in the improvement of consumer products, so I'd like to ask you a few questions about beer.

There is no response from DUNCAN.

What is your average weekly consumption of beer? Bottles. How many. Per. Week.

DUNCAN: Which year?

MARIAN: Pardon me?

DUNCAN: It varies wildly. In '63 I barely touched a drop. Last year I drank like a fish.

MARIAN: What about this year? So far. Per week.

DUNCAN: *(Thinks hard.)* Ten.

MARIAN: That's excellent.

DUNCAN: It is?

MARIAN: You've crossed the threshhold.

DUNCAN: I have?

MARIAN: Ten qualifies for the survey. May I continue?

DUNCAN: I suppose. Do you want to come in?

MARIAN: I uh oh—

             They enter.

             Do you live here alone?

DUNCAN: It depends what you mean by "alone".

MARIAN: By yourself.

DUNCAN: I have a roommate. Trevor. Don't sit in his chair. In case he comes home. He's very territorial.

             DUNCAN sits and MARIAN remains standing.

             I'm ready for surveying, Miss Seymour.

MARIAN: I'm going to repeat some phrases from our proposed commercial for you, and I want you to tell me what each one makes you think of.

DUNCAN: Free association?

MARIAN: Yes.

DUNCAN: I like that.

MARIAN: "Deep down manly flavour".

DUNCAN: Sweat. Hart House with the rads going full blast. Underground locker rooms and jock straps.

MARIAN: Okay. What about "long cool swallow"?

DUNCAN: It's a bird. White. Falling from a great height. Shot through the heart, in winter. The feathers coming off.

MARIAN: "Tang of the wilderness".

DUNCAN: That's one of those technicolour movies about dogs or horses. Tang is half-dog, half-wolf, and he saves his master three times, once from fire, once from flood, and once from wicked humans. Eventually he gets blasted by a cruel trapper and wept over.

MARIAN: *(Writing madly.)* Fine. Fine. Now the last one. "Healthy, hearty taste"?

DUNCAN: Heartburn. Or no, that can't be right. Wait. Now I see. It's one of those cannibal stories. There's one in the Decameron and a couple in Grimm's—the husband kills the wife's lover or vice versa and cuts out his heart and makes it into a stew and they eat it. There's a scene like it in Shakespeare, too.

MARIAN: *Titus Andronicus.*

DUNCAN: Yes! But whether any of it would go well with your beer I don't know. I never drink the stuff.

MARIAN: You said you drink ten bottles a week!

DUNCAN: Ten's my lucky number. And I was bored; I felt like talking to someone.

MARIAN: But it means I won't be able to count your interview!

DUNCAN: Oh, you enjoyed it. Admit it—all the other answers you've got today were boring. I've livened up your day.

MARIAN: I'd have preferred accurate to lively. Well. Thank you. You've been most helpful. I'll go now.

MARIAN goes to door and half opens it.

DUNCAN: So tell me, why do you have a crummy job like this? I thought only fat sloppy housewives did this sort of thing.

MARIAN: Oh well, we all have to eat, don't we. Besides, what else can you do with a B.A. these days?

MARIAN pushes off DUNCAN and pulls on the Park Plaza set.

(To Audience.) I'm not too confident of Peter's reaction to Len Slank. So I'm creating the optimum

conditions for our meeting—the top of the Park Plaza. It's Peter's natural habitat—the bartenders know him, no one ever gets irresponsibly drunk— and drinking twenty-nine stories up gives you a pleasing sense of the vertical that's rare in this city. I only wish I'd had time for dinner...

PETER appears, bearing drinks.

PETER: Who is he, again?

MARIAN: I told you, he's an old friend from college.

PETER: Why haven't I met him before?

MARIAN: He's just returned from England. He's a TV producer.

PETER: Ah. One of those artsy-craftsy types. Probably queer.

MARIAN: Quite the opposite. He's in News.

PETER: That's OK then.

MARIAN: His major at Trinity College was virgins.

PETER: Did you and he—

MARIAN: God no! I mean, I was a virgin, so technically I was eligible. And one night I think he had, in fact, fixed me in his sights. But I said something ironic—and that was that. There's something about an ironic virgin that takes the fun out of the hunt.

PETER: He sounds like a nasty piece of work.

MARIAN: He's really quite charming. And you're bound to like him—he's dead set against marriage. Which reminds me, how is poor Trigger?

PETER: Pathetic bastard. He looks terrible. Two days ago he was so noble and free. His fiancée—she's a predator. She has sucked him into a domestic void.

MARIAN: You're making her sound like a vacuum cleaner.

PETER laughs.

And maybe it'll turn out to be a good thing. After all, she hasn't exactly robbed the cradle. Isn't Trigger twenty-six?

PETER: I'm twenty-six!

MARIAN: Uh—it's a very different twenty-six.

PETER: Yes it is, isn't it. Marian, I don't know what I'd do if you didn't understand. Most women wouldn't, but you're so sensible.

LEN Slank appears.

LEN: (*Coming close.*) Marian, Marian, so good to see you!

LEN kisses MARIAN on both cheeks.

MARIAN: Where'd you pick that up?

LEN: Pick what up.

MARIAN: The (*Imitates the double kiss.*)

LEN: I've been in Europe.

MARIAN: You've been in England. I love your new accent.

LEN: Oh, do I have an accent? And you my good chap— you are?

MARIAN: This is Peter Wollander. Len Slank.

LEN: Ah yes, Peter the lawyer.

PETER: Still an articling student, technically.

MARIAN: So how was merrie olde England?

LEN: Crowded. And I don't just mean Carnaby Street— that's for hippies. Every time you turn around in London now you bump into somebody from here. It's getting so you might as well not go there at all. But I was sorry to leave.

PETER: Why did you?

MARIAN: You had such a good job there.

LEN: You've got to watch women when they start pursuing you. They're always after you to marry them.

PETER: Bingo!

LEN: You've got to hit and run. Get them before they get you, and then escape.

PETER: Marian tells me you're in television. News.

LEN: Yes. I haven't got anything at the moment but I ought to be able to pick up something here. They need people with my experience.

> *LEN and PETER move off a bit. MARIAN turns to see AINSLEY, who has just entered. AINSLEY has completely re-invented herself as a seventeen year-old virgin.*

            I'd like to see a good commentary programme in this country, I mean a really good one. Though God knows how much red tape you have to go through to get anything done around here.

PETER: Say, do you hunt?

LEN: I have—

PETER: That's great.

> *LEN and PETER see AINSLEY and fall silent.*

            You didn't tell me Ainsley was joining us, Marian.

MARIAN: That's because I didn't know. You *are* Ainsley?

AINSLEY: Gosh, I didn't know this was a bar! I sure hope they don't ask for my birth certificate. Hi Peter.

MARIAN: Len, this apparently *is* Ainsley. My roommate.

LEN: I knew you had a new roommate but you didn't tell me she was so—so young!

MARIAN: Yes, well, I'm sort of keeping an eye on her, for the folks back home.

LEN: May I order you a drink, Ainsley?

AINSLEY: Gosh. Could I have just a glass of ginger ale?

PETER: Ginger ale! Since when (were you a teetotaller?)

AINSLEY: With ice cubes. If they have them.

LEN: Excellent. Garcon! Well, Ainsley. Nice of you to join us.

AINSLEY: *(Looks down demurely.)* Thank you.

LEN: Peter and I had just started talking about hunting—we won't if it will upset you—

PETER: Who—Ainsley? You can say anything in front of her! She's got a mouth like an (open sewer)

AINSLEY: Oh no, I'd like to hear you talk! But gosh, Peter I didn't know you were a hunter! Did you know he was a hunter, Marian?

MARIAN: Gosh, yes, I think I did.

PETER: I *used* to hunt, before Marian. Nothing major. Crows, groundhogs.

AINSLEY: *(Looking at MARIAN.)* Gosh. Crows. Groundhogs.

PETER: Vermin.

MARIAN: Virgins?

            LEN finds this very funny.

PETER: My buddy Trigger and I used to hunt rabbits up north. There's packs of them there. The last time—hard to believe it's been over a year now—my first shot—one shot, nailed one right through the heart.

            PETER and LEN's conversation is mostly inaudible except for the odd phrase that burbles up under

MARIAN's narrative, following. The key phrases that should be heard from the men are in italics.

MARIAN: *(To Audience, over.)* Peter's voice is getting louder and faster. The "quality" of his voice is changing, too.

PETER: (The rest of them got away. Trigger said, "You know how to gut them, you just *slit her down the belly and give a good hard shake* and the guts fall out." I whipped out my knife, German steel, what a mess: *The trees were red for yards.*)

MARIAN: *(To Audience.)* I don't recognize his voice. That crayon Temperance sign flashes in my mind. I can't let my perceptions about Peter be distorted by alcohol.

PETER: (*Rabbit guts dangling from trees.* Trigger and I got good shots of it.)

MARIAN: *(To Audience.)* I study the reflections of the other three as they move on the polished black table top, as in a pool of water. They're all chin and no eyes, except for Ainsley—she's all eyes, aimed demurely downwards.

PETER: (Say, you must know about cameras. *What kind of lens do you use?*)

LEN: (Japanese.)

PETER: (Japanese eh. I'd have thought German.)

LEN: (No, Japanese.)

PETER: (Japanese. It's funny that Trigger and I had the cameras with us at all. *Usually when we hunt we travel light...*)

MARIAN: *(Notices a tear.)* What's this?

At this point MARIAN slides away from table, noticed only by AINSLEY.

I must get a grip. I can't make a fool of myself.

To PETER and LEN, who ignore her.) Excuse me. I'm just going to—powder—

The washroom set moves in—for the first time a set moves without MARIAN's involvement. She notices this, but accepts it. She wipes her eyes.

(To Audience.) I've never done anything like this before. This is absurd! But—why won't Peter talk in his normal voice! He's treating me like some sort of stage prop—silent, solid, two-dimensional. And what do I do about Ainsley? Is it any of my business? If I interfere I'm breaking an unspoken code of the hunt, but it just doesn't seem right. I mean, this is more than a hunt. This is—extraction.

AINSLEY enters.

AINSLEY: Marian. Marian? Are you in there? Are you all right? After fifteen minutes I looked out on the patio for you and then I waited—

MARIAN: Was Peter (asking for me)

AINSLEY: They're engrossed in their guns—or maybe it's their cameras. They seem to be interchangeable.

MARIAN: "Gosh". Getting your own sights set?

AINSLEY: We'll see. I have to find out more about him first. Of course you won't say anything.

MARIAN: I suppose not. Though it doesn't seem ethical. It's like spearing fish by lantern.

AINSLEY: I'm not going to do anything to him. It won't hurt. But what's wrong with you—I saw you start to cry at the table.

MARIAN: You know I can't drink very much. It's probably the humidity. There's a storm coming. I've had a long day. I didn't have time to eat. Let's go back—to your ginger ale.

AINSLEY: I'm dying for Scotch.

MARIAN: Hah—that'll teach you to play under-age.

AINSLEY: Actually, Len's suggested we go to his place.

MARIAN: All four of us?

AINSLEY: Yes. He wants to show Peter his teleconverter. Whatever the hell that is. Something to do with hunting vermin, no doubt. Are you going to be OK?

MARIAN: I'm fine.

MARIAN manages to push in some of LEN's apartment, but some of it appears unbidden. AINSLEY appears with another ginger ale, and follows the men off a bit to admire the teleconverter. They form a tight circle, excluding MARIAN. She sits on the backless couch-bed.

(*To Audience.*) But I'm not fine. I'm aching with fatigue. The noise and sight of Peter and Len engrossed with cameras and lenses, with Ainsley virginally spectating, comes at me like waves. (*Looks behind bed.*) There's something very inviting about that space. The behind-it space. I bet it's quiet back there. It would be less humid.

MARIAN slides down behind the bed. She is wedged between it and the wall.

(*To Audience.*) This will never do. It's too damn uncomfortable. I'll have to go right under.

MARIAN is under the bed now.

(*To Audience.*) OK it's a bit cramped. Pffftt. Dustballs like chunks of bread. Mouldy bread. What a pig Len is. Imagine not sweeping under your bed. But you know, it is kind of nice here. Underground. My private burrow.

PETER: Where's Marian?

LEN: Probably in the loo.

PETER: Oh. So is this your new lens.

LEN: Japanese.

PETER: Japanese eh.

LEN: I'll show you how it works.

MARIAN: *(To Audience.)* I'm going to sneeze. Damn. What possessed me to come under here? I'll be covered in fluff when I come out. How can Peter let me stay down here while he's moving about in the open! And what's happening with us anyway! All summer we've been moving in a certain direction. We don't talk about the future because we're "not involved". Except we are.

                PETER sits down on the bed.

                (External voice.) OW!

PETER: *(Getting back up.)* What the hell!

AINSLEY: Gosh! Someone's under the bed!

PETER: Len, you dirty dog—you've got a girl under there.

AINSLEY: Perhaps it's Marian.

PETER: Marian wouldn't be under the bed.

MARIAN: *(To Audience.)* Yes, I would.

LEN: I think it is Marian.

PETER: Couldn't be. She's too sensible.

MARIAN: *(To Audience.)* No, I'm not.

AINSLEY: This is scaring me!

MARIAN: *(To Audience.)* Oh gosh!

LEN: Peter, she's your girlfriend.

PETER: Marian: are you under the bed?

MARIAN: Yes Peter, I am.

PETER: Why are you under Len's bed?

MARIAN: It's quieter down here.

PETER: Well you better come out now. And then I think it
             will be time for us to go home. So come out.

MARIAN: I can't.

PETER: Why.

MARIAN: I'm stuck.

AINSLEY: Poor Marian!

PETER: You're stuck.

MARIAN: I can't move.

AINSLEY: You men must do something! Len, please, unstick
             her!

PETER: All right then, we're going to lift the bed for you.

LEN: On the count of three—

LEN & PETER: One two three HIKE!

             *They lift the bed a foot or two and MARIAN
             scrabbles out. She stands, removing fluffballs.*

PETER: Now suppose you tell us what you were doing
             under there.

MARIAN: I was visiting dirty dog Len's harem.

PETER: You should have told us you were stuck.

MARIAN: *(Angry.)* I didn't want to interrupt you!

             Pause.

PETER: All rightee. Well Len, pal, Marian and I are going to
             push off now. It's been awfully pleasant. I hope we
             can get together soon. I'd really like to see what you
             think of my tripod.

AINSLEY: I'm coming too.

PETER: No, if you don't mind, Ainsley. Marian and I need to
             talk.

LEN:	I'll get you home safely.

PETER, with MARIAN, walk outside. Distant sound of thunder and flashes of lightning.

PETER:	The car's parked (on Lowther)
MARIAN:	I'm not going back with you. I'll walk home.
PETER:	Do what you like.

MARIAN starts to walk off.

Marian, no. Marian—wait. I can't let you walk home. At least let me drive you—it's not safe, it's going to rain—come to the car—please? Let me—please?

MARIAN acquiesces.

Now perhaps you'll tell me what that nonsense was about.

MARIAN:	It wasn't nonsense and I don't want to discuss it.
PETER:	If you can't hold your liquor you shouldn't drink.
MARIAN:	I wasn't drunk.
PETER:	Then why did you have to ruin a perfectly good evening?
MARIAN:	I don't seem to have ruined it much for you. You were enjoying yourself.
PETER:	Oh, so that's it. We were boring you, and not paying you enough attention, so you had to crawl under the bed. Ainsley behaved herself properly.
MARIAN:	She was acting like a—like a virgin!
PETER:	So?
MARIAN:	So!
PETER:	The trouble with you is, you're rejecting your femininity.

MARIAN:	OH SCREW MY FEMININITY! *(Pause.)* Femininity has nothing to do with it! You were just being plain ordinary rude.
PETER:	I beg your pardon?
MARIAN:	You heard me. Plain—ordinary—rude.
PETER:	I was?
MARIAN:	You were. Rude rude rude!
PETER:	Really?
MARIAN:	Really.
PETER:	I didn't mean to be rude.

Pause.

MARIAN:	I know you didn't. I'm sorry to yell.
PETER:	No, I provoked you with my rudeness. I'm sorry.
MARIAN:	I'm sorry I was rude, too.
PETER:	You weren't rude.
MARIAN:	I was incredibly rude. I yelled.
PETER:	I likely deserved it. I'm truly sorry.
MARIAN:	No, I'm sorry.
PETER:	I guess we're both sorry. There's the first drop. *(Opens umbrella.)* It's a good thing I didn't let you walk home.
MARIAN:	Yes. Thank you.
PETER:	You've still got some fluff in your hair. Here. No, let me. You looked so silly coming out from under that bed. A big giant fluffball, that's what you are. Marian: open your eyes.
MARIAN:	Maybe I am drunk. That must be it. You shouldn't let me drink on an empty stomach. I skipped supper.

PETER: You have to eat, honey.

MARIAN: I know but by the time I'd finished the beer survey
              (and gotten dressed)

PETER: You're a drunk, hungry Silly.

MARIAN: I don't know what I was doing tonight.

PETER: That's OK. Don't worry about it. It was all kind of
              charming, in retrospect. It was so—out of character
              for you.

              (Pause.) Marian.

MARIAN: Yes.

PETER: Marian. *(Pause.)* How do you think we'd get on as...
              How do you think we'd be... If we were married.

                  Crack of thunder, close.

              What do you think. Marian?

                  Lightning, close.

              Marian?

MARIAN: I swear I just saw myself in your eyes—mirrored—
              small and oval—

PETER: Huh? Darling?

MARIAN: I uh—

PETER: I know.

MARIAN: It's a bit out of (the blue)

PETER: Of the blue, yes.

MARIAN: You've only just recovered from Trigger.

PETER: True. But a man's got to settle down sometime, and
              I am twenty-six. It'll be a lot better in the long run for
              my practice, too. The clients like to know you've got
              a wife. And most women are scatterbrained but

you're such a sensible girl. That's the first thing to look for when it comes to choosing a wife. A sensible girl. When would be a good date? For us.

MARIAN: *(Involuntarily and non-sensibly:)* Groundhog Day.

PETER: Pardon me?

MARIAN: Our wedding day? Oh, I'd rather have you decide that. I'd rather leave the big decisions up to you.

            MARIAN directs PETER off and re-establishes her flat.

            (To Audience.) He's changing in front of my very eyes. From a reckless young bachelor into a rescuer from chaos. A provider of stability. "I'd rather leave the big decisions up to you"? I've never said anything remotely like that before. And funny: I think I mean it.

            She crawls in to bed. Black. Instant alarm. It's the next morning; AINSLEY is standing over MARIAN, with a tomato juice and toast.

AINSLEY: I have a hunch you'll need this.

MARIAN: My head feels like—like someone scooped it like a canteloupe and left me the rind to think with.

AINSLEY: Nice.

MARIAN: You obviously survived Len.

AINSLEY: It was like escaping from a giant squid but mostly I did it by acting dumb and scared. That's very necessary at this stage. I made him call a taxi and I got home before you even. But what about you? I was quite worried. You were behaving like a real idiot. Where'd you sleep last night, on top of your bed or under?

MARIAN: Very funny. Peter and I got engaged.

AINSLEY: Get married in the States.

MARIAN:	Why!
AINSLEY:	It'll be so much easier to get the divorce.
MARIAN:	Aren't you supposed to congratulate me? Squeal with vicarious joy?
AINSLEY:	I don't think you know what you're doing.
MARIAN:	Subconsciously I wanted to marry Peter all along.

AINSLEY has pulled out a calendar and is making marks.

But enough about me, apparently. What're you doing now?

AINSLEY:	Figuring out my strategy.
MARIAN:	For the—
AINSLEY:	For the baby.
MARIAN:	I don't know how you can be so cold-blooded about it. And why Len!? He's my friend. It could get complicated. Aren't there lots of others around?
AINSLEY:	Not right now, or at least nobody who's such a good specimen.
MARIAN:	Have you investigated Len's ancestors?
AINSLEY:	We had a short conversation just before he made his pass. He doesn't have any allergies. There don't seem to be any morons on either side of his family. I wanted to find out whether he was Rh Negative but that might have given things away. And he is in television. That means he must have something artistic buried in him.
MARIAN:	You're like a general plotting a major campaign. You don't need a calendar. You need a blueprint of your bedroom. No, no, make that a contour map. You could draw little arrows and dotted lines and an X at the point of conjunction.
AINSLEY:	Please don't be frivolous.

MARIAN: When's it going to be—tomorrow?

AINSLEY: No, it can't be for a while. At least a month. You see, I've got to make sure that the first time will do it.

MARIAN: Why?

AINSLEY: It all depends on his psychology. I can't get too eager; he'll get scared off. As long as he hasn't got me, I can have him whenever I need him. And keeping track of things on the calendar—sure it's like a general. So what. When that night of reckoning with Len comes, it's got to seem accidental. My resistance overcome. It can't look pre-arranged.

MARIAN: Even though it is. *(Gathering laundry.)*

AINSLEY: Exactly. Say, you aren't by any remote chance going to the laundromat today are you?

MARIAN: I was thinking of it—

MARIAN begins pushing out laundromat: washers, dryers and eventually, DUNCAN. AINSLEY has hustled off to get her laundry and returns with a bag, which she hands to MARIAN.

(To Audience.) She has me, of course. Sunday afternoons always hold a special quality of mournful emptiness for me, that dreadful feeling of nothing to do. So I often fill the void—at the laundromat.

MARIAN has finished establishing laundromat. She is lugging her laundry bag over. When she gets there, she notices she has forgotten her soap.

Oh fiddlesticks! (I forgot—)

DUNCAN: You can have some of mine.

MARIAN: Pardon?

DUNCAN: Use my soap.

MARIAN: How'd you know—

              DUNCAN shrugs.

              Thank you. I wish they'd put in a vending machine.

DUNCAN: You don't recognize me, do you.

MARIAN: You look familiar—we've met—

DUNCAN: You're the Seymour Surveys beer lady.

MARIAN: Oh yes—"Tang of the wilderness"—right, right.

DUNCAN: Without your official shell you look sort of exposed.

MARIAN: Is that good or bad?

DUNCAN: Wow! Those panties—are they yours?

MARIAN: My roommate's.

DUNCAN: They didn't look like you.

MARIAN: I've never seen you here before.

DUNCAN: I come here a lot. Sometimes I just have to get out of
              that apartment. It's all right there as long as I have
              something to iron. I like flattening things out.
              Getting rid of wrinkles. It gives me something to do
              with my hands but when I run out of things to iron,
              well, I have to come here, to do another laundry so I
              can, you know, start the cycle all over again. The
              only thing about laundromats is that you're always
              finding other people's pubic hairs in the washers.
              Want some chocolate?

MARIAN: No thanks.

DUNCAN: I don't like it much, either, but I'm trying to quit
              smoking.

              *Time passes. DUNCAN has finished the chocolate
              and lit a cigarette.*

              I like watching my clothes. I watch laundromat
              washers the way other people watch television. It's

soothing because you always know what to expect and you don't have to think about it.

MARIAN: *(Amused.)* I never thought of it that way.

DUNCAN: And I can vary my programmes a little. If I get tired of watching the same stuff I can always put in a pair of green socks or something colourful.

MARIAN: I bet you're a student.

DUNCAN: So's Trevor. My roommate. We're graduate students. In English.

MARIAN: I always thought being a graduate student would be exciting.

DUNCAN: *(Snickers.)* Exciting. It looks exciting when you're an eager undergraduate. You think you're going to find out the real truth in graduate studies. But you don't. Things get pickier and pickier and staler and staler until it all collapses in a welter of commas and shredded footnotes and then, after a while, it's just like anything else. You're stuck in it and you can't get out and you wonder how you got there in the first place. If this were the States I could excuse myself by saying I'm avoiding the draft but, as it is, I've got no good reason.

Time passes.

MARIAN: What's your thesis on?

DUNCAN: 'Pre-Raphaelite pornography'.

MARIAN: There was some?

DUNCAN: I'm hoping so. But right now I'm supposed to be writing an overdue term paper from the year before last. I write a sentence a day. On good days, that is.

MARIAN: What's the term paper on—or have you got to that yet?

DUNCAN: 'Monosyllables in Milton'.

MARIAN: Maybe you're in the wrong business.

DUNCAN: It's too late. Once you've gone this far, you aren't fit
             for anything else. Something happens to your mind.
             You're overqualified and overspecialized and
             everybody knows it.

MARIAN: Oh. Well, I guess that sort of answers that.

             Time passes. They watch their clothes.

DUNCAN: Your oranges are nice. That dress, in particular.

MARIAN: My roommate's.

DUNCAN: Of course.

             Time passes. They watch.

MARIAN: Are you from out of town then?

DUNCAN: Of course, we all are. Nobody really comes from
             here, do they?

             Time passes.

MARIAN: Are you hungry?

DUNCAN: Metaphorically?

MARIAN: I have some pudding samples. You could eat one
             and then I'll survey you. No?

             *Time passes. During DUNCAN's next speech,
             MARIAN will try to eat a pudding, but finds she has
             no appetite for it.*

DUNCAN: The thing is, it's the inertia of it all. You never feel
             you're getting anywhere. You get bogged down.
             Waterlogged. Last week I set fire to the apartment,
             partly on purpose. I just got interested in seeing a
             few flames and some smoke. Trevor said I was mad.
             But Trevor's the real lunatic. He's writing his thesis
             on womb symbols in D.H. Lawrence.

MARIAN: Maybe you should move out.

DUNCAN: I can't afford it. I'm stuck. Oh, we're done.

MARIAN and DUNCAN gather their stuff. MARIAN walks across stage, with DUNCAN following. MARIAN stops. DUNCAN stops. They turn towards each other, both seeming about to say something. They drop their bags to the sidewalk, and begin kissing. They break and turn away from each other at the same time. DUNCAN leaves and MARIAN turns stage centre, and begins re-establishing her bed.

MARIAN: *(To Audience.)* His mouth tasted like cigarettes. Apart from that, and an impression of the thinness and dryness of his body, I can remember no sensation at all.

MARIAN gets in bed. She slowly cocoons in the blanket and the light narrows on her. As she speaks, the other characters slowly assemble around her bed.

(To Audience.) So here I am. It's Labour Day. Friday's skirmish with Landlady over the charred chops seems so long ago. So much has happened: the beer survey, that dreadful evening with Len Slank... Ainsley being a virgin. The couch. So much has happened. Getting engaged... I've been going over that in my mind, and maybe my actions were really more sensible than I thought. My subconscious got ahead of my conscious self. The decision to get married was a bit sudden but, as Peter says, you can't run around indefinitely. I can imagine the expressions on their faces at Seymour Surveys when they hear. But I can't tell them yet. I'll have to keep my job there for a while longer. Till Peter finishes articling at least. Meanwhile, I should do something constructive. Revise the beer questionnaire. Wash my hair. Clean my room. Fold my clothes from yesterday. Make lunch. But what about the man at the laundromat? I kissed him. Maybe that's a kind of lapse, a blank in the ego, like amnesia. And there's very little chance I'll ever run into him again. In a minute I'll get off this bed and walk through

that pool of sunshine. I can't let this entire day
dribble away, relaxing though it is to lie here. It's
like being on a rubber raft, drifting. Oh, but I must
get organized. I have a lot to do. I really, really have
a really lot to do.

> *MARIAN is completely folded into her blanket now.
> The other characters lift up her bed, and carry her off.
> Black.*

End of Act One

Act Two

MARIAN no longer has the ability to move sets; they change around her and she frequently darts out of the way of advancing desks etc. Sometimes the sets appear on their own; other times the various characters push them out.

MARIAN: *(To Audience.)* Marian sits listlessly at her desk at Seymour Surveys. She's stalling on yet another questionnaire about rice pudding. September and October have just flashed by in a daze of impending nuptials and it's either that—or the fact she's skipped breakfast—again—that's making it impossible for Marian to concentrate.

AINSLEY and LUCY push in their desks.

LUCY: Nice doodles.

MARIAN: May I help you with something?

LUCY: I'll say. The coast-to-coast sanitary napkin survey has gone embarrassingly wrong.

MARIAN: I'm not surprised—it's so inappropriate.

AINSLEY: Don't be silly. Even Lucy thinks it's proper nowadays. Don't you, Luce.

LUCY: Well, they do have full page ads in magazines.

AINSLEY: It's good we're getting out in the open and not being so bloody Victorian.

LUCY: However, our western surveyor wasn't careful whose names she selected.

AINSLEY: She used a phone book. Look. This one's got "Tee
                Hee" written on it. From a Lesley Andrews. *Mr.*
                Lesley Andrews. And this one's from a woman—
                but she's ticked "no" in all the boxes.

LUCY: Look at her age—she's over eighty! We're going to
                have to start all over again. Marian? Marian—you
                haven't heard a word—

AINSLEY: She's distracted. *(Hums a few bars of "The Wedding
                March" as she exits.)*

MARIAN: Ainsley!

LUCY: What—what—are you—is she—oh my—oh no—
                Marian—oh Marian—

                *MARIAN grabs LUCY just as the latter is about to
                whoop.*

MARIAN: It isn't to go any further. I don't want anyone here to
                know—

LUCY: You're so lucky! To Peter?

MARIAN: Of course it's to Peter.

LUCY: Oh—you'll be leaving us.

MARIAN: Peter says I can keep working after the wedding if I
                want. But yes, I probably will leave Seymour
                Surveys, eventually.

LUCY: I always thought Peter was a confirmed bachelor!
                That is what you said! You said he went into
                mourning whenever his friends succumbed. How
                did you catch him?

MARIAN: If I knew, I'd tell you. This is all on the q.t.

LUCY: Oh, of course.

MARIAN: I'm serious. You know how The Men Upstairs will
                react.

                The phone rings. LUCY dives for it.

LUCY: Seymour Surveys, may I help you?

PETER: Marian, office voice.

LUCY: This is Lucy.

               Pause.

PETER: Uh, Lucy?

LUCY: Yes?

PETER: Lucy, may I speak to Marian?

LUCY: Yes, she's right here. The lucky lassie. Marian, it's Him.

               MARIAN grabs phone from LUCY. Light up on PETER. LUCY loiters.

MARIAN: Peter?

PETER: Listen honey, I can't make it tonight. A case came up suddenly. I've got to break its back.

MARIAN: That's all right darling. But it would be nice if we could get these things straight before the last minute.

PETER: I told you, it came up suddenly.

MARIAN: Well you needn't bite my head off.

PETER: I wasn't biting your head off.

MARIAN: It felt like you were.

PETER: I didn't mean to. I'm sorry.

MARIAN: No, I'm sorry—

PETER: —You know how much I'd rather see you, but you've got to understand.

MARIAN: Tomorrow, then?

PETER: It'll depend. I'll let you know.

PETER hangs up. Light off him.

MARIAN: *(Remembers LUCY is eavesdropping.)* Well goodbye then, dear. You too. You too.

The apartment and flat furniture begin appearing, pushed in by AINSLEY. MARIAN may be carried off in her chair.

(To Audience.) Marian feels time eddying and curling almost visibly about her feet, rising around her, lifting her body in the office chair and bearing her, slowly and circuitously but with the inevitability of water moving downhill, bearing her towards that not-so-distant-anymore day in late March when, when she will be escorted down the aisle, eddied into Peter, borne into matrimony—

(Finds herself at home.) Oh—but first time bears her home.

(Dialogue voice.) Ainsley, you here?

AINSLEY: Oh hi. *(Looks in MARIAN's bag.)* I thought you gave up chicken.

MARIAN: I did.

AINSLEY: Last week you said, "Its skin is like my arm with goosebumps." Quote, unquote.

MARIAN: I'm going to try again.

AINSLEY: Anyway, why the food? You're going out for dinner with Peter.

MARIAN: I was but now I'm not. Something came up at his office and he has to break its back.

AINSLEY: But—

MARIAN: What!?

AINSLEY: Marian, it has to be tonight!

MARIAN: What does.

AINSLEY: Len Slank. It.

MARIAN: It?

AINSLEY: It! You know! Baby.

MARIAN: Why tonight? You've been seeing him for two months! Why didn't you do it last month!

AINSLEY: I made myself so pure he decided it would take the full eight weeks to deflower me. And how I have suffered! If it isn't tonight, I don't know what I'll do. We're going out to dinner and I thought maybe if I invited him back here for "coffee"...

MARIAN: In other words, you want me to make myself scarce.

AINSLEY: It would be an awful help.

MARIAN: But where can I go?

AINSLEY: Peter's. You're engaged to him—can't you just pop over?

MARIAN: He'll think I'm being possessive.

AINSLEY: What about Lucy?

MARIAN: I can't cope with any more of her envy. I suppose I could see a movie.

AINSLEY: Fabulous idea!

MARIAN: But the movie isn't going to last all night. I'll have to come back around twelve. And Landlady will have something to say, too, if it's past midnight and Leonard Slank is still here.

AINSLEY: Hopefully, the situation will be well under control by then. But just in case, don't go charging through any closed doors without knocking.

MARIAN: Why would I go in your room? Whoah—wait a minute! "Any" closed doors? Now look Ainsley, I draw the line at my own bedroom.

AINSLEY: But it's so much neater than mine! And if I'm being overwhelmed by passion and swept off my feet I can't very well interrupt and say, "You've got the wrong bedroom." I'll hang a tie on the doorknob.

MARIAN: Whose tie?

AINSLEY: Why Len's, of course.

MARIAN: Why not just use his scalp?

> *MARIAN sits watching a movie. It flickers on her face.*

(To Audience.) Marian skips dinner—again—the chicken—*(Shudders.)* and heads to her local cinemas. One has a foreign film with subtitles, advertised outside by black and white fuzzy reproductions, and much use of the words "adult" and "mature" and "award-winning". The other is a low budget American Western. Cowboys and dying Indians. She's looking for shelter—so that's what she chooses. To her relief, it is a real one—not one of those nouveau Westerns in which the cowboys have psychoses.

> *The amplified sound of seed-munching has been rising under the foregoing. DUNCAN's head slowly rises from a seat behind MARIAN. He has been eating seeds. MARIAN has become increasingly distracted. DUNCAN edges over to her. In her ear:*

DUNCAN: Sunflower seeds.

> *He drops out of sight. MARIAN looks around.*

MARIAN: Oh oh—I'm hallucinating. I'm finally going mad. What a nuisance. *(Looks up at house.)* OK. Home. Len Slank. Please, be gone.

> *MARIAN sees a tie dangling victoriously.*

Aw fiddlesticks, where am I going to sleep—

> *The other characters all appear and push in the Seymour Surveys furniture. The phone rings.*

LUCY: Seymour Surveys, may I help—Hello? You want me
                 to do what! Bring my roommate's panties for
                 ironing! Sir. This is a place of business not some
                 some unsanitary panty-ironing bordello! *(Pause.)* I
                 have never met anyone in a laundromat! *(Pause.)* I
                 was doing a beer survey? Labour Day weekend?
                 Oh. You want Marian. *(Holds phone out.)*

MARIAN: Peter?

LUCY: Definitely not.

MARIAN: Seymour Surveys (may I help)

                 Light up on DUNCAN, in his dressing gown.
                 LUCY continues to eavesdrop.

DUNCAN: This is Duncan. From the laundromat.

MARIAN: Oh yes.

DUNCAN: People at your office have unusual phone manners.
                 I'm sorry I startled you in the movie last night but I
                 knew you were dying to know what I was eating.
                 I'm trying to stop smoking and I find seeds helpful.
                 There's a lot of oral satisfaction in cracking them
                 open—

MARIAN: Mr. uh Duncan, I'm sort of at the office and we really
                 don't have time for outside calls.

DUNCAN: But I need you. I—need—you.

                 Pause.

MARIAN: Pardon?

DUNCAN: I need you.

                 Pause.

MARIAN: However, I would like to talk to you. Some more uh
                 convenient time. *(Sotto.)* What do you need me for?

DUNCAN: *(Sotto.)* Ironing. I've already done everything in the
                 house and I thought I'd come over to your house

	and iron some of your things.
MARIAN:	(*Sotto.*) No! Not a good idea! No!
DUNCAN:	(*Sotto.*) But it's urgent!
MARIAN:	I'll uh bring some things to your house. (*For LUCY's benefit.*) The uh documents.
DUNCAN:	Actually, I prefer that. It means I can use my own iron. It makes me uncomfortable to use other people's. But please hurry; I really do need it.
MARIAN:	Yes, as soon as I can after work. About seven. Thank you.

A smallish bag drops to the floor. MARIAN picks it up and turns, into DUNCAN's dim doorway.

DUNCAN:	Got the stuff?
MARIAN:	It's not very much. A few blouses, some guest towels.
DUNCAN:	Well, it's better than nothing.
MARIAN:	Where are you going?
DUNCAN:	To my bedroom. I can't iron out here. Trevor gets nervous whenever he sees me using appliances. I smashed our bathroom mirror last week. With the frying pan. I got tired of being afraid I'd walk in there some morning and I wouldn't see my reflection in it. So I grabbed the frying pan out of the kitchen and gave it a whack. It was a perfectly understandable symbolic gesture—but Trevor was very upset. He was cooking an omelette at the time.
MARIAN:	May I watch you iron, or is that an invasion of privacy?
DUNCAN:	There isn't much to see, but sure. It's probably better for you to come to my room anyway; Trevor doesn't really like intruders mussing up the apartment.
MARIAN:	I don't muss.

DUNCAN: Trevor has high standards. One stray sock can throw him off his womb thesis for weeks.

            DUNCAN sets up the ironing table and pushes out a bed. MARIAN stands beside him, watching.

MARIAN: You're good.

DUNCAN: Of course I'm good.

MARIAN: Men usually can't iron.

DUNCAN: You mean, the men you consort with. *(Burns self.)* Ow! Damn, don't get me talking, I burnt myself. Ow. Ow. Ow? *(Pause.)* Aren't you going to comfort me?

MARIAN: I don't think it's really needed.

DUNCAN: You're right. I'd enjoy it though. And it does hurt. Well. That was a vigorous session but it wasn't enough. Why don't you let me touch up that blouse for you while my iron's still hot. You've missed the sleeves (and collar)

MARIAN: I'm wearing it!

DUNCAN: Take it off.

MARIAN: No.

DUNCAN: Wear my dressing gown. *(Takes it off.)* I'd feel a lot calmer if I could iron your blouse.

MARIAN: (I well uh)

DUNCAN: I'll just touch up the sleeves and collar—I'll turn my back. *(Turns.)* I won't peek, don't worry.

            MARIAN takes off her blouse and hands it to DUNCAN, who immediately starts ironing it. MARIAN takes the dressing gown, puts it on, and sits on DUNCAN's bed.

MARIAN: Just don't burn it. I could never explain that away; I can't leave home with a perfectly good blouse and come home two hours later with iron marks.

DUNCAN: Ironing is like term papers—it's a treadmill. You iron the damn things and then you wear them and they get all wrinkled again.

MARIAN: If they stayed neat you'd apparently have nothing to do.

DUNCAN: Maybe I'd like to do something worthwhile for a change. Production-consumption. What bothers me though is that none of it is ever final—you can't finish anything. I have this great plan for permanent leaves on trees; it's a waste for them having to produce a new lot every year.

MARIAN: Some of the leaves could be white, for winter.

DUNCAN: Yes! Yes. Done. See.

DUNCAN hands blouse back to MARIAN, who is impressed with his work. He continues to the bed, where he lies down beside MARIAN, and closes his eyes. She stares at him. He opens his eyes.

Hey. You sort of look like me in that.

DUNCAN tugs her down to him. He begins stroking her. MARIAN pulls back.

Why'd you do that?

MARIAN: I guess I wonder if you're caressing me, or having a rub of your dressing gown—and I just happen to be inside it.

DUNCAN: It's possible.

MARIAN: I think I ought to tell you something. I'm engaged.

DUNCAN: That's your problem. It's like me telling you I got an 'A' on my pre-Raphaelite pornography paper. It's an interesting fact but it doesn't have much of anything to do with anything.

MARIAN: I shouldn't be here.

DUNCAN: But you are. And I'm glad you told me. It makes me feel a lot safer. I don't want you to think that this means anything. You're just another substitute for the laundromat.

MARIAN: I wonder what you're a substitute for.

DUNCAN: I'm very flexible. I'm the universal substitute.

TREVOR: *(Off.)* Hey Dunk! I'm home! Dunko!

DUNCAN: *(Sitting up.)* Oh hell.

MARIAN: Your roommate?

DUNCAN: Trevor.

MARIAN: (Dunko?)

TREVOR: *(Entering, with bags.)* I've got the chow!

TREVOR barges into bedroom.

Whoah! Duncan! And a Wombperson!

DUNCAN: Hi. We were ironing.

TREVOR: Ironing.

DUNCAN: Yeah.

TREVOR: It doesn't look like ironing. It looks more like pressing. Well, spag and balls in half an hour. Have it all done by then, guy.

TREVOR leaves.

DUNCAN: Damn! Damn Damn—

MARIAN: Why get upset? If anything, it's Trevor's fault for barging in. I suppose we should've hung a tie.

DUNCAN: He thinks he's my parent. He'll think you're corrupting me. He has to be protected from reality. You'll have to go. So I'll see you next Tuesday? Bring some of your room-mate's stuff.

DUNCAN is moving his room off. MARIAN lies back in what is now her bed. Black. Alarm

> *immediately. Lights. AINSLEY is proudly retching.*
> *As MARIAN turns to see her, AINSLEY stands up,*
> *smiling.*

AINSLEY: Oh Marian, did you hear that?!

MARIAN: Yes—

AINSLEY: What an absolutely wonderful way to start the day!

MARIAN: It's not a definite sign, don't (get your hopes up)

AINSLEY: Except I'm late, very late. And things are beginning
                to taste funny—tea is bitter and eggs are sulphury.
                Oh Marian, Marian: you're going to be an aunt!

> *AINSLEY exits for more morning sickness.*

MARIAN: *(Calling after her.)* Well. Well congratulations,
                Ainsley. And for what it's worth, I do think you'll be
                a good—a wonderful mother.

> *MARIAN turns, just as PETER enters, bringing a*
> *restaurant table and two chairs with him. MARIAN*
> *almost falls into one.*

PETER: *(Eating.)* I believe children must be punished for all
                breaches of discipline.

MARIAN: Physically?

PETER: If necessary. Of course, no one should ever strike a
                child in anger; the main thing is to be consistent.

MARIAN: Perhaps they just need understanding.

PETER: Try giving understanding to some of those little
                punks, the motorcycle boys and the dope addicts
                and the draft dodgers up from the States. They have
                no sense of responsibility. They think the world
                owes them a living. That's how they were brought
                up. Nobody kicked the hell out of them when they
                deserved it.

MARIAN: Perhaps someone kicked the hell out of them when
                they didn't deserve it.

PETER: You don't understand, dear. You're a small town girl but Toronto's a big city now—children need more discipline here.

MARIAN: Peter.

PETER: Mm?

MARIAN: Why do you think they keep these restaurants so dark?

PETER: It's romantic, darling.

MARIAN: I bet it's to keep people from seeing each other while they are chewing and swallowing.

PETER: You and your theories. Your food.

            PETER eats. MARIAN will try—but fail.

MARIAN: *(To Audience.)* The non-eating is getting worse. December was a nightmare of discarded turkey. Every time Marian takes laundry over to Duncan's something else goes—last week it was lamb and mutton, after he told her the word 'giddy' came from 'gid'—the loss of equilibrium in sheep caused by worms in their brains. Anything with bone or fibre or tendon. How on earth can Marian manage a mouthful of filet!? This used to be part of a real cow that once moved and ate. And then the cow was killed, knocked on the head as it stood in a queue like someone waiting for a streetcar...

PETER: *(Puts his dish away.)* Wow, I was hungry! A good steak always makes you feel a little more human. But what's the matter darling? You've hardly touched yours.

MARIAN: I don't seem to be hungry anymore. I guess I'm full. Maybe my stomach's too tiny.

PETER: You're a strange, delicate thing.

MARIAN: You don't know the half of it.

            LEN Slank and LANDLADY appear, pushing in

*MARIAN's apartment flat. PETER moves
restaurant set out with MARIAN on it. Again, she
gets off and only just; perhaps as she's just about to
be wheeled right offstage.*

LANDLADY: There's a man up there!

MARIAN: Are you sure?

LANDLADY: Yes. I had to let him in. He was banging on the front
door like a maniac. He's been here before. To see
Miss Tewce. The Child has been thrown right off her
practising.

Exiting.

MARIAN: Thank you—I'll deal with him—

*LANDLADY has exited. MARIAN turns to face
LEN.*

LEN: ...I expect she's told you.

MARIAN: That's she's pregnant. Yes, of course.

LEN: I feel sick about it. I was shocked when she told me.
To have that hit you over the phone. She's such a
little girl, Marian—I mean, most women you'd feel
what the hell, they probably deserve it. But she's so
young! What a mess. What'm I going to do! I mean,
I can't marry her, and—and—birth. Birth terrifies
me. I can't stand the thought of having a baby.

MARIAN: It isn't you who's going to have it.

LEN: Marian, can't you try and reason with her? If only
she'd have an abortion, of course I'll pay for it.

MARIAN: I'm afraid she won't. *(Beat.)* You see, the whole point
of it was that she wanted to get pregnant.

LEN: She what?!

MARIAN: She did it on purpose. She wanted to get pregnant.

LEN: That's ridiculous. Nobody in their right mind wants
to be pregnant.

MARIAN: You'd be surprised. It's quite fashionable these days and Ainsley reads a lot. She was particularily fond of psychology at college.

LEN: She's been to university! I should've known! That's what we get for educating women! They get all kinds of ridiculous ideas!

MARIAN: There's some men that education doesn't do much good for, either. Anyway, don't be upset. You don't have to do anything. Ainsley is quite capable of looking after herself.

LEN: The little slut. Getting me into something like this.

MARIAN: Sssh. Here she comes. Now keep calm. We'll all be adults.

            AINSLEY is entering. She doesn't see LEN.

AINSLEY: Wait till you see what I got! It was such a jam downtown and I had to carry all these groceries— I'm eating for two you know—and look at this knitting book and this adorable wool, baby blue—

MARIAN: So it's going to be a boy.

AINSLEY: Of course. I mean, it would be better if it was male.

MARIAN: Maybe you should have discussed it with the prospective father before you took the necessary steps. Len *(Points.)* may have wanted a girl.

LEN: Marian has explained everything.

AINSLEY: Thanks loads.

MARIAN: He had a right to know.

AINSLEY: Just think, Len, I'm going to be a mother! I'm really so happy about it.

LEN: Well I'm not so damn happy about it! All along you've been using me. What a moron I was to think you were sweet and innocent when it turns out the whole time you were—college-educated! You weren't interested in me at all! The only thing you wanted from me was my body!

AINSLEY: And what did you want from me?! Anyway, you can keep your peace of mind. I'm not threatening you with a paternity suit.

LEN: Peace of mind, hah. Oh no, you've involved me—psychologically. I'll have to think of myself as a father now. It's indecent. I'm going to be all mentally tangled up in birth. Gestation. Fecundity.

AINSLEY: You're displaying the classic symptoms of uterus envy. Where the hell do you think you came from, anyway! You were all curled up inside somebody's womb for nine months.

LEN: Don't remind me! I really can't stand it. *(Breaking down.)* She made me do it! She made me!

AINSLEY: I didn't "make" you (do anything)

LEN: Mummy made me.

AINSLEY: Huh?

LEN: Mummy made me! Mummy made me do it.

AINSLEY: Mummy? Len—is there something in your family history I should know?

MARIAN: Ainsley—I'll deal with this.

AINSLEY: But this could be important genetic information.

MARIAN: Go to your room, now!

AINSLEY: But—

MARIAN: GO! GO!

              AINSLEY, startled, leaves.

              OK, Ainsley's gone. Try and get control of yourself. What exactly did your mummy make you do?

LEN: We were having eggs for breakfast and I opened mine and there was uh uh I swear there was a uh a little chicken inside it. It wasn't born yet. I didn't want to touch it but she didn't see, she didn't see what was really there and she made me eat it. "Eat your eggy, Lenny." So I had to oh oh I can't stand it.

MARIAN: There, there. It's not going to be a little chicken anyway. It's going to be a nice lovely baby. A lovely baby boy apparently. Now let's get your coat and you can (get some fresh air...)

MARIAN and LEN move off. LUCY and AINSLEY appear and move on the Seymour Surveys furniture.

(To Audience.) And the next morning—sure enough—Marian opens her own soft-boiled egg and sees the yolk looking up at her with its one accusing yellow eye. She finds her mouth closing together like a frightened sea anemone. "It's living, it's alive," the muscles in her throat say, and tighten. She pushes the dish away. Her conscious mind is becoming used to the procedure. *(Aloud.)* There's almost nothing left!

MARIAN sits glumly at her Seymour desk. A 'Congratulations' streamer may fall over her and LUCY and AINSLEY enter with platters of food.

What on earth?

AINSLEY: *(Sotto.)* Sorry Marian—I couldn't stop them.

LUCY: *(Dinging a glass.)* There's jelly, almond, peanut butter and honey sandwiches. Warning, warning: Mrs Grot's Orange-Pineapple Sponge Delight will go straight to your hips! But before we eat up, girls, I must make an announcement! Quiet! Quiet please. Little gatherings like these come but rarely, and only once in a lifetime for most of us. Never, for some of us.

Sound of Oh?'s ring out.

Yes. Yes, it's official. The rumours are true! Marian is taking The Big Step with Peter!

Oohs of curiosity.

She has been ringed!

Envious Ooh chorus.

Show us your rock, Marian.

Curious chorus of anticipatory Oh's. MARIAN has to find it and put it on. She flashes it dutifully. Sound of admiring Ooohs.

And I'm sure we'll all wish Marian the very best in her new life. By the way—Marian's Peter—is a lawyer!

More Oohs, jealous this time. MARIAN has receded under her coat. The Oohs turn to wind. MARIAN stands up and walks away, while the others remove the Seymour Surveys furniture. DUNCAN pushes on a park bench. He is well-mufflered.

MARIAN: *(To Audience.)* Marian cannot possibly confront her apartment. Ainsley will come home and take up her infernal booty-knitting and there are still the wedding invitations... She gets off the subway at Eaton's College Street and trudges west to one of her favourite sanctuaries, Queen's Park. It's a huge dimly-white island in the darkness of late afternoon.

MARIAN sits down, ignoring DUNCAN.

DUNCAN: Panties feeling wrinkled?

MARIAN: Pardon me?

DUNCAN: Marian! It's me!

MARIAN: Duncan? I wasn't expecting—you're covered in snow!

DUNCAN: It was snowing.

MARIAN: You'll freeze.

DUNCAN: I might. Freeze with me. If you're cold you can come under my coat. Here.

MARIAN undoes the buttons of DUNCAN's overcoat and huddles inside it.

You took a long time getting here. But I knew you'd come by. Call it male intuition. *(Pause.)* Marian: I've been thinking it might be a good idea if we went to bed.

MARIAN: *(Coming out from under DUNCAN's coat, in surprise.)* That's impossible! I'm getting married in a less than a month!

DUNCAN: That's your problem. It has nothing to do with me. And it's me I thought going to bed would be a good idea for.

MARIAN: And why might that be?

DUNCAN: I mean, you don't exactly arouse a raging lust in me or anything. But I thought you would know how, and you'd be competent and sensible about it. It would be good if I could get over this thing I have about sex.

MARIAN: What thing?

DUNCAN: I think I'm a latent homosexual. Or maybe I'm a latent heterosexual. Whichever; I'm pretty latent. I've taken a number of stabs at it but, well, it's like when I'm supposed to be writing term papers I think about sex, but when I've finally got some lovely backed into a corner and everybody's ready for the coup de grace—

MARIAN: You start thinking about term papers?

DUNCAN: Yes!

MARIAN: What makes you think sex would be any different with me?

DUNCAN: Maybe it wouldn't. But at least you won't get hysterical. You're not insulted are you?

MARIAN: It's a bit impersonal. But that's kind of a relief. When Peter tells me he loves me, I have to say something back. He requires exertion. You certainly don't need any of that.

DUNCAN: The thing is, I'd like something to be real. Not everything, that's impossible, but maybe one or two things. I mean, Dr. Johnson refuted the theory of the unreality of matter by kicking a stone, but I can't go around kicking Trevor.

MARIAN: And anyway, what if your foot's unreal?

DUNCAN: Exactly.

MARIAN: All right, Duncan. Suppose we did go to bed. Just theoretically. We can't go to my place.

DUNCAN: Nor mine. Not with Trevor being so paternal.

MARIAN: We'd have to go to a hotel. As a married couple.

DUNCAN: They'd never believe it. I don't look married. Hey— we could go to the kind of hotel where we don't have to be married!

MARIAN: You want me to pose as—as a prostitute?

DUNCAN: Why not.

               MARIAN shakes her head.

               Well, that's that. Maybe I'm incorruptible. *(Sigh.)* I'll walk you back to the subway. You probably have to go home and finish your invitations.

MARIAN: How'd you know?

DUNCAN: You've been complaining about them for three months now.

MARIAN: I guess I have. Wait. Duncan—will I see you after I'm married?

DUNCAN: I don't know.

MARIAN: I could bring you ironing. Couldn't I?

DUNCAN: Sure, I'll still need that, won't I.

            DUNCAN disappears. MARIAN returns to her apartment, where AINSLEY is pacing.

AINSLEY: Where've you been! Why did you rush out of the party!?

MARIAN: It was too dire—I know Lucy means well but— *(Notices AINSLEY has been crying.)* What's the matter?

AINSLEY: I went to Pre-Natal after work. And I was so happy and I was doing my knitting and everything during the first speaker. He was talking about the advantages of breast feeding. There's even an association for it now. But then they had this psychologist and he talked about the Father Image. He says children ought to grow up with a strong Father Image in the home.

MARIAN: You knew that before, didn't you?

AINSLEY: Oh no Marian, it's really a lot more drastic! He has all kinds of statistics and everything. They've proved it scientifically. If I have a little boy, he's certain to turn into a homosexual!

MARIAN: Nonsense.

AINSLEY: It's in every psychology textbook. No father figure: homo-sexual.

MARIAN: If having no father figure is the cause of it, then nine out of every ten men would be homosexual. And the other ten percent would wish they were.

AINSLEY: Please don't make light of this.

MARIAN: Well you're being an idiot. OK, sorry. Perhaps I could lend Peter.

AINSLEY: I don't want that kind of Father Image! Peter? Oh God no, (the very idea)

MARIAN: Peter may not want that kind of child! Anyway, leave Peter out of this!

AINSLEY: (You brought him up)

MARIAN: It's always Peter this, Peter that with you—LEAVE
              THE POOR BASTARD ALONE!

AINSLEY: I was just joking—

MARIAN: Well it's not funny! Sorry. I'm sorry to yell. It was
              rude. It's bridal nerves.

AINSLEY: Is everything OK—with you and the poor bastard?
              Sorry, sorry Peter—

MARIAN: Everything is fine. And let's get this straight—I can
              call him "poor bastard" but you can't. It's a term of
              endearment. And no, everything isn't fine. It isn't
              fine at all. Nothing is fine. I'm beginning to wonder
              if I'm normal. Do you think I'm normal?

AINSLEY: Not in the least.

              MARIAN groans.

              But you're sensible.

MARIAN: If only I was! Something has been happening to me
              these past few months. Since summer. I can't eat
              certain things.

AINSLEY: I know exactly what you mean—being pregnant—
              (there's a whole list)

MARIAN: No, it isn't that I don't like the taste. It's more
              serious. I can't eat any meat, and eggs... And now
              vegetables! Carrots! It's a root. It grows in the
              ground and sends up leaves. Someone digs it up—
              does it scream? And does it die right away or is it
              living and screaming so low I can't hear?

AINSLEY: Wow. Marian, isn't this something you should
              resolve before you get hitched? Talk to Peter.

              *PETER is pushing his apartment on. MARIAN lies
              backwards, into PETER's lap. He is reading.*

MARIAN: Peter?

PETER: Mmm.

MARIAN: Peter dear.

PETER: Mmm.

MARIAN: Peter! Peter dear, am I normal?

PETER: You're marvellously normal, darling.

            PETER goes back to his paper. MARIAN sighs and sits up.

            Oh, are you getting up? I could use another drink. Could you flip the record too, that's a good girl. And then we should make plans for my party next week. My final party.

MARIAN: Final?

PETER: As a free man, silly! Marian?

MARIAN: Yes.

PETER: I'm going to invite some of the men from the firm. *(Beat.)* It's important we make a good impression.

MARIAN: We meaning me? I could buy a dress—

PETER: Something zippy. And perhaps you could *(Touches her hair.)*

            MARIAN moves away. The actors playing LUCY and DUNCAN appear in hairdressers' smocks and work on MARIAN as she talks—installing and spraying her new hairdo, and presenting her with the red dress.

MARIAN: *(To Audience.)* So, the day of the party, Marian goes to the beauty parlour. A stylist takes her usually straight hair and draws it up into a mod shape, embellishing it with two tusk-like spitcurls projecting forward. Then cements everything in place with hairspray. It's as if Marian's head is now a cake! Iced and ornamented! Thus lacquered, Marian buys a new dress, one that is not camouflage but red and short and sequined. And then she returns home...

Voices rising. MARIAN enters her apartment.

AINSLEY: You've got to come in here and talk to Len! You've got to make him listen to reason! Oh, I like your hair.

MARIAN: Hi Len.

LEN: My God Marian, after all this woman has done to me—now she wants me to marry her! Yeah, I like it too.

AINSLEY: What's the matter with you anyway? You don't want a homosexual son, do you!

LEN: Goddamn it, I don't want any son at all!

AINSLEY: I'm going to have the baby and it should be under the best possible circumstances and it is your responsibility to provide it with a father image.

LEN: I'm not going to marry you. And don't give me that responsibility stuff. You deliberately allowed me to get myself drunk, and then you seduced me.

AINSLEY: You thought you were seducing me! And after all, that's important too. Your motives. Suppose you really had been seducing me and I'd got pregnant accidentally. You'd be responsible then!

LEN: You're like all the rest of them. Stick to the facts, you sophist.

MARIAN: Could we please be a little less noisy! You might be heard by Landlady!

LEN: OH SCREW YOUR LANDLADY!

LANDLADY appears.

LANDLADY: WELL! This is a pretty pass.

LEN: *(To AINSLEY.)* You and your goddamn fertility worship can go straight to hell! *(To LANDLADY.)* Who are you?

LANDLADY: I own this house and I have a young daughter.

AINSLEY: Don't tell him that! Even your hulking thing won't be safe.

LANDLADY: Miss Tewce, I have had (enough of your)

LEN: All you clawed scaley bloody predatory whoring bitches can go straight to hell! All of you! Underneath you're all the same! But you'll never get me! Never! Never!

             LEN storms out. The others are temporarily silenced.

MARIAN: I really don't think he's going to come around.

AINSLEY: I'll simply have to find another father figure. Is there something we can help you with?

LANDLADY: Miss Tewce. I have always tried to avoid scenes and unpleasantness but now I'm afraid you'll have to go. The drinking was bad enough—I know all those bottles were yours and I'm sure Miss McAlpin never drinks. I do like your hair. I'm a tolerant person. I turned the other way when that horrid young man was here—overnight. Thank goodness The Child is innocent to these matters. But to make it so public, dragging your disreputable drunken friends into the open. In broad daylight, for all to see!

AINSLEY: Hah! You're just worried about what the neighbours will say. Well, I consider that immoral. And I'd like you to know that I'm going to have a child, too.

LANDLADY: WHAT!

AINSLEY: *(With pride.)* A homosexual. And I certainly wouldn't choose to bring him up in this house—you're the most anti-creative life-force person I've ever met. I'll be pleased to move. I don't want you exerting any negative pre-natal influences. Now get the hell out of our flat; Marian and I have an orgy to prepare for.

Black on LANDLADY. AINSLEY turns to MARIAN and begins prepping her for the party, helping her into the dress etc.

AINSLEY: Have you eaten anything at all?

MARIAN: I had a vitamin pill.

AINSLEY: God Marian, that's not enough.

MARIAN: I looked in the fridge. The freezer won't open for ice. I was going to have tea—but all the cups are dirty or, worse, they're in the sink, covered with organic water.

AINSLEY: Sorry. Hey—I really like your dress.

MARIAN: Truth is, I don't know if I can face the party. Peter's friends are nice enough but they don't know me; I'm afraid of losing my shape.

AINSLEY: (Your shape?)

MARIAN: I'm afraid I'll spread out—I won't be able to contain myself. Maybe I should invite a few people, from my side.

AINSLEY: I'm from your side. I'll come.

MARIAN: Oh, thank you Ains. And maybe Lucy.

LUCY: *(Appears on the phone.)* It's awfully short notice, Marian.

MARIAN: Yes, I apologize for that. But you see, I'd been under the impression that everyone was going to be married—but now Peter tells me there'll be several unescorted bachelors. Things get so dull for single men at parties.

LUCY: —Give me the address!

Light off LUCY and up on DUNCAN.

MARIAN: It's me. Marian.

DUNCAN: Oh.

MARIAN: Would you like to come to a party tonight? At Peter's place? I know it's late but—

DUNCAN: Trevor and I are supposed to be going to a brain-picking graduate English party.

MARIAN: Maybe you could come after your brains are picked. And do bring Trevor. Please, Duncan. I won't know anybody there. I need you to come.

DUNCAN: No you don't. But maybe we'll come anyway. It would be sort of a kick to see what you're getting married to. Bye.

             DUNCAN hangs up. Light off him.

MARIAN: I'm going over to help Peter set up. See you later? Promise?

AINSLEY: I'll be there. Marian?

MARIAN: Mm?

AINSLEY: You look amazing.

             Light up on PETER, who is prepping the party. He stops and sizes MARIAN up.

PETER: In a word: wow.

             PETER unzips and zips MARIAN's dress playfully.

             And I really like your hair.

MARIAN: They'll be here any second.

PETER: So what.

MARIAN: We don't have the ice out yet.

PETER: *(Zipping MARIAN back up.)* Right. Ice. There'll be plenty of time for the other later.

MARIAN: Peter.

PETER: Mm.

MARIAN: Peter, do you love me?

PETER: I'm marrying you in three weeks, aren't I?

MARIAN: Peter!

PETER: Of course I love you, don't be silly. And I especially love Red Woman.

MARIAN: Darling, I hope you don't mind—I've invited a few more people. Ainsley, Clara and Joe, some graduate students, oh, and the Office Virgin—

PETER: The Office what?

MARIAN: Lucy.

PETER: Lucy's a virgin?

MARIAN: Apparently.

PETER: Well, that'll make Len happy.

MARIAN: Len Slank?

PETER: Yes, I ran into Len this afternoon and invited him. He said yes but I don't know—he looked really rough around the edges.

MARIAN: You really asked Len?

PETER: Telepathy. I must have sensed you were inviting virgins.

MARIAN: Ooh boy.

            There is a knock on the door.

PETER: Someone's early.

            MARIAN goes for the door.

LUCY: *(Entering; craning neck.)* Hi Marian where are the bachelors. Is that one, is that a bachelor? He's kind of handsome, though in a plain sort of way. I mean, if I close my eyes I bet can't remember what he looks like. *(Closes eyes and tries to imagine.)* Nope. *(Opens them again.)* Now I remember. Ooh, he's handsome. *(Closes eyes.)* Nope, I've forgotten again. *(Opens.)* Ooh, he's handsome.

MARIAN: That's my Peter.

LUCY: Oh you're so lucky.

MARIAN: The bachelors aren't here yet. Peter? This is Lucy. Lucy's my boss.

LUCY: *(Coy with PETER.)* Hardly. The Men Upstairs are the bosses. I'm just the—liaison.

PETER: Pleased to meet you.

MARIAN: You can put your coat in the bedroom.

LUCY exits. PETER gathers MARIAN in his arms.

PETER: I want you to wear red every day of our married life. *(Breaks off.)* Darling, it's almost zero hour, but before they all come I'd like a couple shots of you. There's only a few exposures left on this roll, and I want to put a new one in for the party. Lean against the wall—could you stand any more stiffly? Don't hunch your shoulders like that. Stick out your chest. Smile Marian.

Knock on door; MARIAN bolts for it.

Damn, here they are.

MARIAN opens the door. A wild-looking LEN is there, holding a bottle.

LEN: You'll never get me.

MARIAN slams the door shut. Breathes. Opens it again.

She made me do it.

MARIAN: I know, I know. Come in, Len.

LEN: She's a predatory whoring bitch!

MARIAN: Len, you have to behave.

PETER: Hey pal, looks like you've got a headstart!

MARIAN: Perhaps Len could have something to drink—
               something non-alcoholic? (And food—)

PETER: Come with me, buddy—

LEN: *(Moving off with PETER.)* I need a lawyer.

PETER: You've come to the right place. There'll be ten here
               tonight.

               *Another knock on the door. MARIAN answers. A
               multitude of guests have arrived. MARIAN almost
               falls back into the room at the sight of them, but
               recovers. She speaks above a growing babble:*

MARIAN: *(To Audience.)* And then they begin arriving, fast
               and furious, like pans of hard cookies banged out
               from shiny dough. They rap and enter, rap and
               enter, young and satisfied, sleek and smiling,
               cavity-free, laundered, soaped, shampooed,
               cologned, pressed to perfection. First a lawyer then
               another, then another and another, all of them with
               wives who glisten and clutch their husbands' arms
               like stuffed barnacles, baked trophies, the spoils of
               war, lawyer wife lawyer wife lawyer wife lawyer
               wife

               *LUCY reappears, a bit drunk, and pulls MARIAN
               aside.*

LUCY: They are all in couples! I counted. Ten men. Ten
               women. All in pairs. You promised me bachelors!

               LEN lurches out of the kitchen.

               Oh—but what's that?

LEN: You're just a bunch of scaley, predatory—

LUCY: Ah!

LEN: Man-eating, fertility-worshippers!

LUCY: How forceful!

PETER: *(Pursuing him.)* Len pal, let's get some food into you.

                PETER pulls LEN back into the kitchen.

LUCY: Was he a bachelor?

MARIAN: Yes, but not a very nice one—Lucy, Lucy, come
                back!

                *LUCY exits to the kitchen. The sounds of the party
                have risen considerably. MARIAN stands centre
                stage, and holds out her arms. She twirls slowly amid
                the noise. Knocking on the door will start.*

                (To Audience.) The party rages. Marian stands alone.
                A vision in red. So much of her has been added and
                altered. Marian's arms are the only portion of her
                flesh that is without a nylon or leather or varnish
                covering. And even they look fake, like white
                rubber or—or boneless plastic. But what lies
                beneath the surface? What's holding it together?

                *MARIAN twirls a bit more and practises smiling.
                The sound of knocking becomes audible.*

PETER: Marian—the door?

MARIAN: Sorry.

PETER: And honey, you forgot to put out the pickled
                mushrooms.

                MARIAN heads for the kitchen.

                No dear, get the door.

                MARIAN turns and goes to the door. She opens it.

TREVOR: Is this the right number? Apartment Twelve Oh
                Four, The Manitoba? Marian?

MARIAN: Yes Trevor, it's me. I'm so glad you could come.

                TREVOR enters.

	Duncan—are you coming in?
DUNCAN:	You didn't tell me it was a masquerade. Who the hell are you supposed to be?
TREVOR:	Duncan has taken a rude pill.
MARIAN:	Please (come in)
DUNCAN:	Forget it.
MARIAN:	I really want you to meet Peter. That's him. Over there, with the camera.

During this, PETER has been trying to line up LEN Slank and take his picture.

DUNCAN:	I can't. It would be a bad thing. One of us is sure to evaporate. It would probably be me. It's too loud in there. *(Leaving.)* I couldn't take it.
MARIAN:	Where are you going?
DUNCAN:	Goodbye! Have a nice marriage!

DUNCAN exits.

| MARIAN: | Duncan! |
| TREVOR: | He seems to have disappeared. |

Starts to leave.

MARIAN:	Stay. *(Steering TREVOR to the kitchen.)* The Office Virgin is expecting you.
TREVOR:	The Office what? *(Has exited.)*
PETER:	*(To LEN.)* Let's get some food in you. Here. Marian arranged these. Women are so much better at arranging things on plates.
LEN:	Like men's heads.
PETER:	That's funny, Len. Those are pigs in blankets—or would you prefer a devilled egg?
LEN:	*(Backing up.)* No. No eggs. No. No eggies.

PETER: Well smile, at least. Marian, come stand beside Len. *(Sotto.)* Hold him up. Come on Len, be a sport— smile for the camera—

LEN: No more pictures. No. No.

              LEN backs into LUCY.

LUCY: Are you a goddamn bachelor?

LEN: Live free or die.

LUCY: Prove it. Show me your fing ringer. *(Sees.)* Excellent. I'm Lucy. That's Lucy with a u. *(Laughs at her joke.)* I mean, a u instead of two o's. *(Another laugh.)* Lucy or Loosey? Lucy Goosey.

              LUCY gooses LEN, who flees. LUCY pursues him.

              Hey Mr. Bachelor: Marian says you're in television. Black and white—or colour? That's a joke! Come back here!

              There's another knock on the door. MARIAN answers. It's AINSLEY, wearing orange again. The dress is tighter now.

AINSLEY: Sorry I'm late. I couldn't decide what to wear.

MARIAN: Len's here.

AINSLEY: Oh.

MARIAN: He's drunk. Peter invited him. I'm sorry. If you want to go I'll understand.

AINSLEY: *(Sweeping in.)* It doesn't matter to me in the least. After this afternoon, there's nothing he could say that would disturb me.

MARIAN: But he seems quite upset—

AINSLEY: Not my concern—

MARIAN: OK, but I don't want you to say anything to him that'll upset him even more. The party must run smoothly.

AINSLEY: So these are Peter's friends. Are you OK?

MARIAN: Yes, yes—

LEN: *(Has moved in.)* Well I'm not. I'm not OK at all.

AINSLEY: Yes, we know you aren't.

LEN: I'm about as un-OK as a man can get.

AINSLEY: Go away.

MARIAN: (Len)

AINSLEY: Shoo.

LEN: You'll never get me.

MARIAN: Len, please.

LEN: You'll never, ever get me!

AINSLEY: Oh, we'll see about that. Attention. Attention everyone! Stop the music!

                The noise subsides.

MARIAN: Ainsley, don't.

AINSLEY: Attention! Len Slank and I have a marvellous announcement!

PETER: *(With camera.)* Wait—let me focus!

AINSLEY: We're going to have a baby!

PETER: Len—you dirty dog!

MARIAN: This isn't (the right time.)

LEN: You rotten bitch! That's right folks, and now we're going to have the christening, in the midst of this friendly little gathering. Baptism in utero. I hereby name it after me. Baby Len!

                LEN empties his beer over AINSLEY. There's a mixed reaction from the crowd; mostly they think Len is being convivial. LEN quickly hurries out.

MARIAN: I'm so sorry—Peter invited him; I never thought he'd behave like that!

A pause. Focus on AINSLEY; her lip begins to tremble and she starts to cry. TREVOR steps up immediately, rips off his woolly turtleneck revealing a surprisingly muscular torso thickly matted with hair. Or not. He covers AINSLEY with his sweater.

TREVOR: Allow me. We wouldn't want you to catch a chill. Not in your delicate condition.

AINSLEY: Thank you, gallant sir. I don't believe we've met.

TREVOR: I'm Trevor.

AINSLEY: I'm Ainsley.

TREVOR: You're damp. Womb-baby's damp, too.

AINSLEY: Perhaps we could go somewhere more private, where there are towels.

TREVOR and AINSLEY exit. Party sounds continue under MARIAN's narration. As she speaks, the apartment disappears and the laundromat rolls in.

MARIAN: *(To Audience.)* Marian's coping but she knows it won't last. There's too much noise, too much laughter, too much everything. She's swaying and smiling and feeling like a two-dimensional thing, a paperwoman from a mail-order catalogue. She should never have worn red—it makes her a perfect target. She has to get out of the party before it is too late—before she does something that shows Peter in a bad light. And herself. She has to do something. *(Realizes.)* She has to get to Duncan. *(To herself.)* He'll know what to do. OK get my coat, my coat where is it? Now keep calm—keep calm—just get to the laundromat—

MARIAN is now at the laundromat.

Duncan? Duncan? Duncan, I'm here.

DUNCAN appears from behind a washer.

DUNCAN: So you are. The Scarlet Woman.

MARIAN: I couldn't stay there any longer. I had to come and find you.

DUNCAN: Why?

MARIAN: Because I want to be with you.

DUNCAN: You should be back there, with what's his name. The man with no features. It's your duty. He needs you.

MARIAN: You need me.

DUNCAN: No I don't. And you definitely don't need me. In fact, none of us needs each (other)

MARIAN: Can't we just go someplace?

DUNCAN: What's wrong with hanging out here (watching clothes)

MARIAN: That isn't what I mean!

               Pause.

DUNCAN: Oh. Oh that! You mean, tonight's the night? It's now or never? We certainly can't go to my place. Trevor would go insane.

MARIAN: And my Landlady's on the warpath.

DUNCAN: We could stay here. It suggests interesting possibilities. Maybe inside one of the machines. We could hang your dress over the window to keep out the dirty old men.

MARIAN: For God's sakes, come on! Oh fiddlesticks! I don't have any money!

DUNCAN: I do, I think.

               DUNCAN starts pulling things out of his pockets. He eventually finds some bills.

OK, so it definitely won't be the King Eddy. Or any place around here. Can you walk in those?

MARIAN: Of course.

DUNCAN: I suppose you spent years in training. You probably went to a finishing school for high-heeling.

MARIAN: Shut up and walk.

A bed wheels on and maybe a flashing neon light. A bare bulb may descend.

DUNCAN: Wow—this place is amazing. Did you see how the night clerk looked at you!

MARIAN: Yes.

DUNCAN: Well, what do we do now? You must know.

MARIAN: We get in bed as quickly as possible. This room is freezing.

DUNCAN: Look at this ashtray! "A gift from Burk's Falls"! "Made in Japan"!

MARIAN: Put down that damned ashtray, take off your clothes and get into that bed.

DUNCAN: Oh all right.

MARIAN: Now!

DUNCAN tears off most of his clothes and hops into bed. He stares out at MARIAN, who is struggling with her dress.

Get back out of there and unzip me.

DUNCAN gets back out and starts to unzip MARIAN.

DUNCAN: Hey! What's that!

MARIAN: What's what.

DUNCAN: Is that a corset?

MARIAN: It's a girdle.

DUNCAN: I've never got this far in real life. Can I look at it? God, how medieval. How can you stand it!

MARIAN: Get back in bed!

DUNCAN gets back in; pulls over most of the covers. There's a tussle as MARIAN tries to get in.

I'm freezing dammit! Duncan! Let me in!

MARIAN gets in and snaps off light. Silence.

DUNCAN: Is this the part where I crush you in my manly arms?

MARIAN: No, we think about term papers.

DUNCAN: That's mean.

MARIAN: I'm sorry. Crush me.

There are some gropings, then gradual silence. Time passes. Morning light invades. MARIAN gets up and begins dressing.

(*To Audience.*) Last night everything seemed resolved. But this morning she can't remember what that resolution was. Whatever decision she made is already forgotten—if indeed she had ever really decided anything. It might've been an illusion—like the blue light on their skins last night. (*Of DUNCAN.*) Oh he's accomplished something—but she hasn't. And Peter is still real—very, very real.

DUNCAN's head emerges.

How do I get out of this mess!

DUNCAN: It ought to be obvious I'm the last person you should be asking. Anyway, I thought you were the capable type.

MARIAN: I am. I was.

DUNCAN: Some would say it's all in your head.

MARIAN: Of course it's all in my head. What I want to know is—how do I get it out? Maybe I should see a psychiatrist.

DUNCAN: He'd only want to adjust you.

MARIAN: I want to be adjusted! I don't see any point in being unstable. And I've been starving myself to death; I don't see any point in that, either. I just want to be safe. I think I must have thought Peter was safety and now I know I've spent all these months getting nowhere. I haven't accomplished anything! Now I've got to decide what I'm going to do.

DUNCAN: Well, don't ask me—it's your problem.

MARIAN: Could you come back with me and talk to Peter?

            DUNCAN is leaving.

            Duncan?

DUNCAN: This is your problem. You invented it—you have to think up your own way out.

            DUNCAN has left.

MARIAN: Wait! I can't do it alone! I don't know what to say! He's not going to understand! No matter what words I end up using. There are no words for this! *(Starts to get it.)* There are no words. There are no— maybe that's it.

            MARIAN returns home to her flat, which has been re-assembled. The phone is ringing.

            Hello?

PETER: *(On phone.)* Where the hell have you been! I've been phoning everywhere! All morning!

MARIAN: I've been somewhere else. Sort of out.

PETER: Why the hell did you leave the party! You really disrupted the evening for me! All of a sudden you were gone! I couldn't make a big production of it,

	with all my colleagues there, but afterwards I looked all over, I called you a dozen times.
MARIAN:	Peter, please don't be upset. There have been no catastrophes. There is absolutely nothing to get upset about.
PETER:	You can't go wandering the streets at night! You might get raped—why don't you think of other people's feelings for a change!?
MARIAN:	What time is it?
PETER:	Two-thirty. Why don't you know the time?
MARIAN:	Peter, I want you to come over later. We can talk.
PETER:	Why can't we talk now!?
MARIAN:	I need to clean up. Be here at five-thirty. For tea and explanations.

MARIAN hangs up. Black on PETER.

| MARIAN: | *(To Audience, as she bakes cake.)* What Marian needs is something that avoids words; she doesn't want to get tangled up in discussion. That way she can know what is real; a test, simple and direct as litmus paper. There is no need for a grocery list. She knows what she needs to buy. *(Grocery bag appears.)* It's all at her supermarket. Her only dilemma, once she begins baking, is if her cake is to be sponge or angel food. She decides on sponge; it seems more fitting. *(Removes cake from oven.)* As soon as it cools, she begins to operate. She makes a head. Nips in the waist. Makes strips for arms and legs. Sponge cake is easy to mold. She ices it, draws on a mouth, eyes, gives it a ruffled dress. Careful, baroque hair with tusk-like spit curls. And finally, she is done. *(Admires her handiwork.)* You look delicious. Very appetizing. *(Noise on stairs.)* |
| MARIAN: | Fiddlesticks—he's here already— |

AINSLEY, then TREVOR enter.

AINSLEY: You're back!

MARIAN: Yes. Oh, hi Trevor.

TREVOR: Hello—

AINSLEY: Where were you last night?

MARIAN: It's a long, long story. Where were you?

AINSLEY: Here.

MARIAN: But Peter said he phoned all night—

AINSLEY: Trevor and I were—busy. What have you got there?

MARIAN: It's a surprise for Peter—listen, he's coming over any minute—you can't stay—

AINSLEY: That's OK, we're kind of in a rush anyway. *(Exiting.)* I'll get the suitcase—

            AINSLEY has left to get suitcase.

MARIAN: Why are you in a rush?

TREVOR: I'll let Ainsley tell you. That sure smells good—

            AINSLEY is returning with suitcase.

MARIAN: What's your news?

AINSLEY: We're getting married!

MARIAN: Oh. That's—wonderful. In the States?

TREVOR: Yes—and then we're honeymooning at Niagara Falls. Listen, I'd love to chat but the bus—we can't miss our bus—

TREVOR: *(Taking suitcase.)* Let me. You mustn't carry anything in your condition—

AINSLEY: *(Kisses MARIAN.)* Be happy for us, Marian.

            AINSLEY and TREVOR are hurrying off.

MARIAN: I am. I am.

AINSLEY and TREVOR have exited.

AINSLEY: *(From off.)* I'll call you when we get back!

LANDLADY: *(Off.)* Miss Tewce! Keep your voice down! The
                 Child—

MARIAN shuts door. She leans against it.

MARIAN: Marian—is—hungry. She actually thinks she could
                 eat something. *(Eyes cake, which still has not been seen
                 by audience.)* But not you. You are about to serve a
                 higher purpose.

LANDLADY: *(Off.)* Who are you!?

PETER: *(Off.)* I'm visiting Marian— *(Calling.)* Marian!

LANDLADY: *(Off.)* Why is everyone yelling!

There is a knock on the door.

MARIAN: Just a minute!

MARIAN straightens her dress and hair etc.

OK. This is it.

MARIAN runs to the cake.

Come in!

PETER: Marian? *(Entering.)* Marian? Where was Ainsley off
                 to in such a rush—Marian—

*MARIAN approaches PETER holding the cake,
reverentially. This is the first time the cake is seen.*

What're you doing? What's this?

MARIAN: It's a cake.

PETER: I know it's a cake, dammit. Why are you still in that
                 dress?

MARIAN: I thought you liked me in red. You know, it's funny.
                 Now that I see you again—I guess I was hysterical

last night. I saw you as a hunter—and I was your target. But you're really not the enemy after all.

PETER: What on earth—

MARIAN: You're actually a normal human being.

PETER: Of course I'm a normal human being. Put that damn (cake down)

MARIAN: Everything is going to be all right. It's just that here, now, in the afternoon light—you look so harmless. But it's really just a test for me, I think. Because the other reality is not so benign.

PETER: You're flipping out—

MARIAN: You've been trying to destroy me. Assimiliate me. But now I've baked you a substitute. Something you'll like much better. This is what you really wanted all along, isn't it. A lovely, spongy, perfect cake woman you can (gobble up)

PETER: Are you on a trip?

MARIAN: Not the kind you think. Shall I get you a fork?

PETER: This isn't a joke. This isn't funny.

MARIAN: Definitely not. Now—some tea?

PETER: Marian!?

MARIAN: The kitchen is a bit of a mess but I'm sure I can rustle up something.

PETER: (Backing up.) No. No tea. No cake. Stay there. No. Don't move. I'll let myself out.

MARIAN: But Peter—you can't leave without having (some cake)

PETER: Really, I can just—I'll let myself out. You were such a sensible girl, Marian.

MARIAN: I still am. Please. Have a slice. At least have a leg.

PETER: You've changed. *(As MARIAN proffers cake.)* No. No!
                I don't want any. Marian. I'll just—I can leave on my
                own. I uh—Marian?

MARIAN: Yes dear?

PETER: Goodbye.

                PETER leaves. MARIAN looks down at the cake.

MARIAN: Oh. Fiddlesticks. That didn't quite turn out the way
                I'd expected. He didn't eat you. Well, as a symbol,
                you're not as tempting as I thought. And I really
                don't think he understood. But—he's gone. *(Sigh of
                relief or release.)*

                (To Audience.) Well. I think—I think I'll clean the
                apartment. I've really let things go this past while
                and of course Ainsley never cleans. And it's
                Sunday, I could do a laundry. Or—or I could write a
                questionnaire or two. Or I could—I—I could—

                DUNCAN appears.

                Oh! What're you doing here?

DUNCAN: Where's Trevor?

MARIAN: Hello to you, too.

DUNCAN: He hasn't been home. What happened?

MARIAN: Oh, it's all off. With Peter.

DUNCAN: I mean, what's happened with Trevor?

MARIAN: *(Expresses exasperation, then:)* He's eloped with
                Ainsley. They're getting married.

DUNCAN: But why?

MARIAN: Why do these things ever happen? They met at the
                party. They hit it off. Ainsley was looking for a
                father figure and Trevor will make an excellent one.
                You trained him well.

DUNCAN: Trevor's abandoning his responsibilities.

MARIAN: What—to graduate school?

DUNCAN: To me!

MARIAN: Oh fiddlesticks!

DUNCAN: What am I going to do?

MARIAN: I haven't the faintest idea. And you know
               something? I don't really care. In fact, I think my
               own situation right now is a lot more interesting
               than yours. I'm hungry. I think I'm hungry for
               steak!

DUNCAN: You're back to so-called reality. You're a consumer.
               I didn't know you could bake.

MARIAN: Yes, I like to, whenever I have the time. After all,
               what else can you do with a B.A. these days?

DUNCAN: It looks very good.

MARIAN: Yes, she does. *(Produces knife.)* Have her head.
               (Whacks off head.) Here—try it—

               MARIAN serves DUNCAN a piece.

               (To Audience.) I watch him eat the cake, the smiling
               pink mouth first, then the nose and then one eye. For
               a moment there's nothing left of the face but the last
               green eye, then it too vanishes—like a wink. It gives
               me a peculiar sense of satisfaction to see him eat, as
               if the work—the baking—hadn't been wasted after
               all.

               *MARIAN smiles at DUNCAN. He smiles back at
               her. Takes a last bite.*

DUNCAN: It wasn't half bad.

MARIAN: Take some home with you. *(Moves away a bit.)*

DUNCAN: Don't mind if I do; it was delicious. Very, very
               delicious.

MARIAN: Duncan?

DUNCAN: Yes?

MARIAN: It was nothing. Really. *(To herself.)* Really. *(To audience.)* Really.

               MARIAN reaches for a bite of cake. Black.

               The End